Five Pillars of the Spiritual Life

A Practical Guide to Prayer for Active People

Five Pillars of the Spiritual Life

A Practical Guide to Prayer for Active People

Fr. Robert Spitzer

Abridged Edition

Ignatius Press–Augustine Institute
San Francisco   Greenwood Village, CO

Ignatius Press Distribution
1915 Aster Rd
Sycamore, IL 60178
Tel: (630) 246-2204
www.ignatius.com

Augustine Institute
6160 S. Syracuse Way, Suite 310
Greenwood Village, CO 80111
Tel: (866) 767-3155
www.augustineinstitute.org

Cover Design: Devin Schadt

Cover Concept: Riz Boncan Marsella

Cover photograph from istockphoto.com

Original edition © 2008, Ignatius Press
ISBN: 978-1-58617-201-5
All rights reserved.

Printed in Canada

Contents

In loving memory of my mother,
whose faith inspired my spiritual life;
and to my novice master,
Father Gordon Moreland, S.J.,
who prepared me well for the journey.

ACKNOWLEDGMENTS

I give thanks to the Father, Son, and Holy Spirit, Whose inspiration and love have guided me steadily on the way to true Home in Them.

I am most grateful, once again, to Camille De Blasi Pauley, who not only transformed these thoughts into writing, but also provided excellent pedagogical and spiritual insight. Her tireless dedication and hours of work have made this volume, as well as so many others, into a publishable reality.

I would also like to thank the Society of Jesus for its patient instruction in the spiritual life, for thirty-two years of spiritual direction, and for providing me with the time to pray.

I am also grateful to Tim Busch and the Magis Institute for organizing the Los Angeles prayer breakfast, which provided the impetus for this book.

Introduction

Saint Ignatius of Loyola, the founder of the Jesuits, espoused the ideal of becoming "contemplatives in action." He was convinced that contemplation (the deep awareness and appropriation of the unconditional Love of God) should affect our actions, and that our actions need to be brought back to contemplation. I believe that there are five essential means through which this ideal can be attained, particularly for busy people: (1) the Holy Eucharist, (2) spontaneous prayer, (3) the Beatitudes, (4) partnership with the Holy Spirit, and (5) the contemplative life itself.

These five dimensions of the spiritual life generally do not develop simultaneously or even in parallel ways. Some develop very quickly but do not achieve significant depth, while others develop quite slowly but seem to be almost unending in the depth of wisdom, trust, hope, virtue, and love they engender. All of them can become habits (second nature), and all are complementary. Hence, even in the midst of sporadic and lopsided development, mutual and habitual reinforcement occurs. The best way of explaining this is to look at each of the pillars individually.

Before doing this, however, it is indispensable for each of us to acknowledge (at least intellectually) the fundamental basis for Christian contemplation, namely, the unconditional Love of God. Jesus taught us to address God as *Abba* (affectionate, caring, supporting parent—literally, "my [loving] Father" or even "Daddy"). This address was, for the people of His time, too familiar for God, too presumptuous for the Master of the Universe, and so Jesus seems to be the first to have uttered it. Yet, when He did so, He made it the center of His theology and the basis for His identity as "Beloved Son."

If God really is *Abba*; if Jesus' Passion and Eucharist are confirmations of that unconditional Love; if God really did so love the world that He sent His only begotten Son into the world not to condemn us, but to save us and bring us to eternal life (see Jn 3:16-19); if nothing really can separate us from the love of God in Christ Jesus (Rom 8:31-39); and if God really has prepared us to grasp fully "with all the saints what is the breadth and length and height and depth, and to know the love of Christ which surpasses knowledge, that [we] may be filled with all the *fulness of God*" (Eph 3:18–20, emphasis added), then God's love is unconditional, and it is, therefore, the foundation for unconditional trust and unconditional hope. It is the full expression of the purpose of our lives, and therefore the goal of our lives. The confirmation and understanding of this truth about God is one of the main fruits of the spiritual life, indeed, of my spiritual life. There can be nothing more important than contemplating, affirming, appropriating, and living in this Unconditional Love. This is the purpose of contemplation, indeed, the purpose of the spiritual life itself.

Chapter One

First Pillar: The Holy Eucharist

Introduction

The Eucharist is *the* center of Catholic spiritual life. It is Christ's unconditionally loving presence healing us, transforming us, unifying us, and granting us peace. The preciousness of this gift cannot be underestimated. There are three facets of the Eucharist that require discussion:

1. The institution and grace of the Eucharist
2. The Eucharist as universal prayer
3. The Eucharist in its relationship to the liturgy and other sacraments

I. The Institution and Grace of the Eucharist

Jesus set His face resolutely toward Jerusalem in the midst of His disciples' warning about impending persecution because He had a plan—a plan to give away His unconditionally healing and reconciling love to the world for all generations. His plan is best expressed in considering His Eucharistic words. When He said, "This is my Body which will be given up for you," the Greek word used to translate His Hebrew (*zeh baśari*) or Aramaic (*den bisri*) was *sôma* instead of *sarx*. *Sarx* means "flesh" and would certainly refer to Jesus' *corporeal* body given on the Cross, while *sôma* is much broader and refers to the *whole* person (mind, soul, will, as well as corporeal body). Thus, *sôma* is much like the word "body" in "everybody" or "somebody" in English. It might, therefore, be roughly translated as "person" or "self." If we substitute the word "self" for "body" in the Eucharistic words, we obtain, "This is my whole self given up for you." This is remarkably close to Jesus' definition of love ("gift of self"—"greater love has no man than this, that a man lay down his life for his friends" [Jn 15:13]). Thus, in the Eucharist, Jesus is not only giving us His whole self—His whole person—He is also giving us His love, indeed, His *unconditional* Love—that is, a love that cannot be exceeded.

This unconditional Love is corroborated by the gift of His blood (which, according to Jewish custom, is separated from the body of the sacrificial offering). When Jesus offered His blood separately from His body, He showed Himself to be an intentional self-sacrifice that He interpreted to be an offering of unconditional Love.

Blood (the principle of life for the Israelites) was the vehicle through which atonement occurred in sin or guilt offerings (which is most poignantly described in the ceremony of the scapegoat on the day of atonement). Jesus' reference to His sacrificial blood would almost inevitably be seen as the blood of a sin offering—with the notable exception that the sin offering is no longer an animal (for example, a scapegoat), but, rather, Jesus Himself, "the Beloved One of *Abba*." Jesus humbled Himself (taking the place of an animal—a sacrificial sin offering) as the Beloved One of the Father, to absolve the sin of the world forever.

Jesus goes beyond this by associating Himself with the paschal lamb. His use of blood within the context of the Passover supper shows that He intended to take the place of the Passover lamb. He loved us so much that He desired to become the new Passover sacrifice, replacing an unblemished lamb with His own divine presence.

You may recall that the blood of the Passover lamb (put on the doorposts of every Israelite household) was the instrument through which the Israelite people were protected from death (the angel of death passing over those houses), which enabled them to move out of slavery into freedom (from Egypt into the promised land). When Jesus took the place of a sacrificial animal, He replaced the situational dimension of the Passover (Egypt) with an unconditional and eternal Love. Thus, He made His self-sacrifice the new vehicle for protection from *all* death (for all eternity) by outshining sin and darkness with His unconditionally loving eternal light.

There is yet a third dimension of Jesus' use of blood that He explicitly states as "the blood of the covenant." A covenant was a solemn promise that bound parties to an inextricable (guaranteed) agreement. (Written contracts were *extremely* rare during Jesus' time.) When Jesus associates His blood with the covenant, He is *guaranteeing* the "absolution from sin," "freedom from slavery and darkness," and eternal life given through His unconditional Love. By referencing the blood of the *covenant*, Jesus makes a solemn and unconditionally guaranteed promise of eternal life and love through Him.

What does Jesus intend this total gift of Himself will bring? Peace, transformation, and unification both now and (unconditionally) in the kingdom to come. I can attest to the remarkable efficacy of all three of these graces in my own life.

With respect to peace, I can remember going to Mass with very disturbing thoughts in my mind (having received bad news, or having been criticized or irritated by someone's actions, etc.). I carried the "tape playing" and emotional discharge associated with those things right into the Mass with me—which sometimes provoked an intensification of internal disturbance during the Mass. But many, many have been the times when a deep calm (beyond myself) replaced that disturbance as I approached and received the Holy Eucharist. I have difficulty attributing this change of condition to mere self-delusion, because wishful thinking has never overcome "intense disturbance" in any other circumstance in my life. Why the Holy Eucharist? Why so frequently? Hmm. . . .

With respect to transformation, in my junior year of college I decided to begin attending daily Mass because of the encouragement of some friends. I was not at the same level of humility and generosity as those friends (indeed, I had some deep-seated utilitarian, egotistical, and materialistic tendencies). Nevertheless, I felt attracted to the prospect through my faith. After about a year, my friends began to comment that I "had really changed." I told them (quite sincerely) that I had not—I was "the same old person." It seemed I was the only one who had not noticed the gradual but cumulative change that had occurred in my heart. I had always said that rationality could be trusted but the emotions could not. This had the unfortunate effect of producing affective and social retardation, but I nevertheless thought it to be true. Now, in retrospect, I attribute my discovery and re-appropriation of my heart to the gradual transformative influence of the Holy Eucharist. I do not consider this incredible life-giving discovery to have arisen out of normal maturation (I was anything but normal), nor do I attribute it to something desired or willed (because I really did not want a heart—I did not trust my emotions), nor do I attribute it to appropriating the emotional conditions of the people around me (because I did not "hang around" the daily Mass group). Rather, I believe that the Eucharist battered my heart or, perhaps better, prepared my heart for the simple exposure to the Word of God, and to the love of God manifest through others at Mass. Slowly but surely Christ's presence and love turned me toward the grace to which I could not bring myself. I received a heart, not a completed heart, but a "foundational heart" opening upon a deeper and deeper appropriation of the unconditional Love, which is the purpose of my life.

With respect to unification, Saint Paul says that we are all united in the mystical body of Christ (see 1 Cor 10:16–17); that is, we share in and derive strength from the grace, love, and joy of the whole communion of saints both past and present. I really had no idea what this meant when I was twelve years old, but I remember one particular Christmas when we had completed opening our presents and my siblings and I were going to Mass with my mother. I felt an unusually acute happiness that I could not ignore, and so I told my mother, "Mom, I'm feeling very happy, but I'm not sure why." She said in reply, "Well, you probably received all the presents you wanted." For some reason, I knew that it was not material happiness (coming from possession of a gift, consumption of food, playing games, and so forth), so I told her, "Mom, I did get all the presents I wanted, but that's not what's making me *this* happy." She thought about that for a while, and then, with a great deal of hope, said, "Well, maybe you're growing up and thinking of things beyond presents.

Maybe you're happy because you've grown to appreciate your family and you had a really intense experience of them at Christmas." I said in reply, "Uhhh, family? I don't really think that's it" (even though I had a really great family). So my mother thought about it some more and then said, as if inspired, "Well, maybe it's the joy of the whole communion of saints on this Christmastide coursing through your veins." I have no idea why she said this, or why I knew it was correct, but I said, "Yep, that's why I think I'm happy." To this day, that childlike response to my mother's deeply insightful remark seems to me to be truth. It is the truth about the communion of saints and the truth about the unifying power of the Eucharist. It is the truth about the love and joy of the whole communion of saints, past and present, coursing through our spiritual veins.

Years later, I had a flashback to that Christmas when I was sitting with my family at my sister's house on Easter. My little niece Kristen was a little more than a year old, and she was sitting in the middle of a crowd of us in some rigged-up chair. Someone told a humorous story that made everybody laugh, and Kristen (who did not understand a word of it) began to laugh as well. As I looked upon her empathetically sharing in the delight of everyone else, taking sublime joy in something that she could not discursively understand, I flashed back to the Christmas of the "joy of the whole communion of saints" through the Eucharist many years before.

The Eucharist truly is the center of our lives as Catholics and Christians. It is the unconditional Love of Jesus Christ unto the peace, transformation, and unification that not only lends stability but unity and finality to our lives. Saint Ignatius saw this and encouraged daily Mass, a habit that has transformed the heart of the Church in literally billions of ways. If it is at all possible, I recommend that everyone, even in the midst of your frenetic activity, find ways to receive the Holy Eucharist during the week. It will bring a consolation leading to greater peace, efficacy, and leadership; a transformation toward the heart of Christ beyond our highest expectation; and a unity with the mystical body, which will impart an indelible stab of joy in our present lives and memories.

II. The Eucharist as Universal Prayer

There can be little doubt that Jesus intended the Eucharist to be both a universal and unifying gift. Saint Paul understood and interpreted this aspect of the Eucharist in his notion of the one body of Christ:

> The cup of blessing which we bless, is it not a participation in the blood of Christ? . . . Because there is one bread, we who are many are one body, for we all partake of one bread. (1 Cor 10:16–17)

Saint John makes the universal character of this unifying body of Christ even more explicit: "For the bread of God is that which comes down from heaven, and gives life to the *world*" (Jn 6:33, emphasis added). "World," here, refers to the whole human community, which is the proper recipient of the bread from *heaven.*

The themes of "unity of believers" and "life for the world" were picked up by the early Church Fathers where the Eucharist was considered to be the communion between the faithful and their bishop. Saint Ignatius of Antioch, for example, exhorts his followers in multiple letters to maintain unity among themselves, meeting together in the Eucharist under the bishop as their head. This theme was further emphasized in later encyclicals (for example, Pope Pius XII, *Mystici Corporis Christi*, paragraphs 19 and 51; Pope Paul VI, *Mysterium Fidei*, paragraph 70; and Pope John Paul II, *Ecclesia de Eucharistia*). Thus, the Eucharist is the occasion to pray for the local Church community, the worldwide Church community, and the life of the world.

As noted above, the Eucharist is a remarkably beautiful and efficacious gift of *personal* transformation and life. Yet It cannot be held to the domain of the personal. By the intention of Jesus, and therefore by Its nature (Unconditional Love), It reaches out to the whole world. It gives life to those in spiritual and temporal need, It unifies the Church in Its life-giving nature and mission, and It moves through the Church to the rest of the world.

Thus, when we receive the Holy Eucharist, we not only pray for personal transformation; we pray for the Church, the unity of the Church, the life of the world, and the Church reaching out to the world in its spiritual and temporal need. This is why the Prayers of the Faithful (in the Mass) include prayers for the Church, the local community, and the world. This unifying and universal aspect is also manifest in all the Eucharistic prayers, where we pray for the Church throughout the world. We also acknowledge that the Lamb of God takes away the sins of the world. The Liturgy of the Hours (the Divine Office) joins itself to the Eucharistic liturgy and prays for the intentions of the Church and the world during morning and evening prayer. This shows the Eucharist to be a central personal devotion that reaches out beyond Itself to the Church, the whole Mystical Body, and the world.

As will be noted in chapter 3, when we offer up our prayers, works, joys, and sufferings of the day, we do it in imitation of

Jesus, Who explained the efficacy of this in His final words on the Cross: "My God, my God, why have you forsaken me?" (Mt 27:46). These words are a reference to the *whole* of Psalm 22, where it is clear that the psalmist (and Jesus) are offering their sufferings as a gift of self to the Father ("gift of self" means "unconditional love") so that *all* people (the world) might come to the Lord:

> The afflicted shall eat and be satisfied; those who seek him shall praise the LORD! May your hearts live for ever! All the ends of the earth shall remember and turn to the LORD, and all the families of the nations shall worship before him. (Ps 22:26–27)

Jesus' self-offering on the Cross (the gift in the Eucharist) is His whole person (His unconditional Love) given for the sake of all peoples, promising good news for the poor.

Mother Teresa understood well the universal and unifying power of the Eucharist within her ministry to the poor and the sick. She received the Holy Eucharist every morning before she went out to serve the poor. The healing power of the Eucharist seemed to flow through her, and the very bodies of the people she worked with mystically resembled the very Body of Christ she had received in the Eucharist: "I realize that when I touch the odorous and oozing members of a leper, I am touching the body of Christ, just as I take His body in the Sacrament of the Eucharist."

Thus, when we receive the Eucharist (with Its peace, forgiveness, healing, and transformation) in our *personal* lives, we should also offer this most precious gift for the Church and her unity, and for the life of the world (particularly those in spiritual and temporal need). When we do this, we can be sure that the Father will honor our offering just as He honored the offering of His Son in giving His life and love to the world. When we offer our reception of the Eucharist for the Church and the "world in need," Christ's love works through our participation in His mystical body, and the grace and benefit that this offering bestows on the world comes back to us as a blessing from all the people we have held in our hearts. This blessing is rich indeed, for it brings us into solidarity with the Church throughout the world and the "world in need," which brings the reciprocal nature of that love back to us. There is a profound beauty here, not only in being mindful of those in need, not only in sharing Christ's love with them, but also in receiving their unique and precious blessing into us. In Christ's mystical body every blessing given is a blessing received.

III. The Eucharist and the Liturgy

The Eucharist's unifying, healing, and transformational power is brought more fully alive through the liturgy in which It is embedded. Its healing power is linked to the Penitential Rite; Its unifying power to the prayers for the Church and the world; Its inspirational and transformational powers to the Liturgy of the Word; Its communion to the congregation; Its splendor to the beauty of song and action; Its transcendent meaning to the liturgical symbols and the architecture of the church; Its "continuity with the past life of the Church" to Its traditions; and Its "continuity with the kingdom of heaven" to the Eucharistic prayers.

Jesus' action at the Last Supper was simple, but the profundity of this action caused later generations to layer on additional elements of splendor in order to express its magnificence. The liturgy not only brings the community together, it not only connects the congregation to the Church and to Jesus; it tries to express the magnificence of Jesus' unconditional Love through the Penitential Rite, the Liturgy of the Word, the Eucharistic Prayer, and all the other elements (ranging from music to vestments to church architecture) that make our hearts soar.

The liturgy also provides the context for *communal* worship and praise. Individual worship (prayer) emphasizes intimacy and depth, while communal worship emphasizes complementarity, community, and breadth. The liturgy contains *both* communal and individual worship, for the Eucharistic Prayer (communal praise) is complemented by the deep, individual intimacy of receiving the Holy Eucharist; the communal praise of the Gloria is complemented by the individual's contrition in the Penitential Rite; the Word of God and the homily are addressed to the group but appropriated individually. The liturgy is a masterwork of communal and individual worship in their reinforcing and synergistic complementarity, a symphony of breadth and depth opening itself to the grace of God through the group to the individual, and through the individual to the group.

IV. The Eucharist and the Other Sacraments

The Eucharist interacts with the other sacraments of the Church. Volumes have been written about the interrelationship between the Eucharist and the sacraments of Baptism, Penance, the Anointing of the Sick, Confirmation, Marriage, and, of course, Holy Orders. The objective, here, is not to write another volume on the interrelationship among the sacraments, but rather to encourage you to expand your thinking about the Eucharist in two respects:

1. To see the Eucharist as the ongoing empowerment of the grace of your Baptism, Confirmation, and Marriage or Holy Orders (through the unconditional Love of Jesus Christ)
2. To receive the sacrament of Penance as a focus and complement to the healing and transformative power of the Eucharist. Think of the sacrament of Penance as liberating the full healing power of the Eucharist through its particular action and grace.

This complementarity between the Eucharist and the sacrament of Penance is most powerfully manifest in our attempts to move through the stages on life's way. As will be more fully explained in the Epilogue, most people move through four levels of desire, and this movement is not easy. A brief explanation here will be sufficient to make some basic points about the efficacy of the sacraments.

The first and most basic level of desire (in Latin, *laetus*) comes from an external stimulus. It interacts with one or more of the five senses and gives immediate gratification, but does not last very long. A sensorial pleasure like an ice cream cone or a possession like a new car can impart immediate gratification from these stimuli.

The second level of desire (in Latin, *felix*) comes from ego-gratification. *Ego* in Latin means "I." This kind of happiness comes whenever I can shift the locus of control from the outer world to myself. Hence, whenever I win, gain power or control, increase in status, or gain admiration or popularity, I feel happy. I feel as if my inner world is expanding. My control relative to the outer world is enhanced.

We also desire love, truth, goodness, beauty, and being. These desires initially manifest themselves as a desire to contribute. The second kind of desire seeks to shift the locus of control to the self. In the third level of desire (in Latin, *beatus*) we try to invest in the world beyond ourselves. We want to make a difference with our lives, time, energy, and talent.

Strange as it may seem, the third level of desire still does not exhaust the scope of human potential, for humans not only desire *some* love, goodness, truth, beauty, and being; they also desire *unconditional, perfect, ultimate*, and even *unrestricted* Love, Goodness, Truth, Beauty, and Being. In the context of faith, one might call this the desire for God. But even if one does not have faith, one can treat it as an awareness of a seemingly unconditioned horizon surrounding human curiosity, creativity, spirit, and achievement. This particular desire differentiates humans from all other animals. In Latin, this fourth level of desire is called *sublimis.*

Residual attachments to Level 1 (material possessions and physical pleasures) and Level 2 (ego-gratification and comparative advantage) can result in frustration, failed resolve, and a host of distressing affective states. Grace (through the power of prayer) can help us through these very difficult times of transition. In my view, the most powerful conduit of grace in such times is the combination of the Holy Eucharist and the sacrament of Penance. There is something about the combination of the graces in these two sacraments that restores resolve, builds patience and peace, grants courage and strength, and manifests the presence of Christ in our lives so powerfully that we resist any urge to give up the pursuit of life in Christ. Christ's presence through the combination of these two sacraments outshines cynicism, discouragement, and desolation; it gives us strength to run the race and to finish the course.

Summary

I now return to the fundamental truth about the Holy Eucharist. Within the context of Its universal and unifying power, within the context of the liturgy and the other sacraments, within the context of the Church through which It is offered, It is the unconditional Love of Jesus Christ given on the Cross to bring us the fullness of His peace, forgiveness, healing, and transformation unto eternal life. It is Jesus, our scapegoat, paschal lamb, blood of the covenant, and Son of God given for our lives and the life of the world. His mystery is infinite in breadth and His love is infinite in depth. For this reason, the Eucharist is the central pillar of the spiritual life of the Church, and that is why Saint Ignatius recommended its frequent reception.

Chapter Two

Second Pillar: Spontaneous Prayer

Introduction

Spontaneous prayers are short, effective, "easy to remember" vehicles for grace in daily life. If we are to avail ourselves of the grace that God wants to give us, we should have a variety of these at hand for use in times of trial, forgiveness, temptation, etc. I will speak of four groups of spontaneous prayers: (1) prayers in times of trial, suffering, and anxiety, (2) prayers to ask for forgiveness, (3) prayers to offer forgiveness, and (4) the "all-purpose" prayer: "Thy will be done."

I. Prayers in Times of Trial, Suffering, and Anxiety

The first and most important prayer here is "Help." We oftentimes forget it because we think it is too easy, or that God would not respond to something that simple; but if God really is Unconditional Love, and God not only hears us but wants to help us in our time of need, then the prayer "Help" should be more than sufficient to evoke a myriad of unexpected graces from the heart of God. This prayer can further (and beneficially) be made more specific by a variety of other prayers. I will here mention only four that have been very important in my own life.

• *The Hail Mary.* For some reason, this prayer has not only been a foundational contemplative prayer (see chapter 7, section VIII), but also one of galvanizing grace in times of trouble. Our Blessed Mother's consoling presence seems to be evoked (along with her help) during the most desperate of times. This prayer, when repeated, opens upon a consolation filled at once with familial strength, a mother's understanding, and the assistance for a "child not fully in control." It seems to activate a providence (a conspiracy of grace) that betokens a mother's request of her son, much like the wedding feast at Cana (see Jn 2:1).

Countless have been the times when it has come naturally to my mind, inviting me to repeat it. Countless too, have been the times when that repetition has led to increasing peace of mind and clarity of thought. I do not know why, but it always seems to give me courage—the courage to do what is right, to face adversaries, to move ahead with unpopular plans, and to bear the possibility of defeat bravely. Why should this occur through a mother's prayer? Yet it does, and I am the living proof of it. Hmm. . . .

• *"Lord, make good come out of this suffering."* Sometimes trials turn into suffering, and sometimes suffering has neither speedy relief nor obvious meaning. At these times, it is essential to ask for the Lord's help to optimize the good in suffering (good for oneself, good for others, good for the community, even good for the mystical body of Christ). Suffering can be debilitating and depressing if we do not see any good coming from it. However, if we recognize a good in suffering for ourselves, others, the culture, the community, and even the mystical body of Christ, suffering can become not only meaningful, but an invaluable companion in the life of grace, virtue, and salvation. The above prayer has helped me to invoke the Lord's blessings upon my suffering (and to recognize that blessing) in the deepest ways.

When I first became aware of the onset of a serious eye problem six months before my ordination to the priesthood, I was completely baffled. Fortunately, I knew that God's providential love would be operative through this challenge throughout the rest of my life. In that faith, I began to pray, "Lord, do not waste one scintilla of this suffering. Make some good come out of it for me (a change in life direction, a deepening of faith and love, a protection from other adversity), for others (a zeal for Your kingdom, a desire to help others, an empathy with those in need, and an eagerness to serve the kingdom), for the culture, and for the community. Lord, optimize the good that can come from this suffering." The Lord has certainly answered this prayer, for He has deepened my sense of gratitude for what I *do* have; He has helped me to see that every day and every moment counts in manifesting His love and presence; He has made me far more circumspect about what matters and doesn't matter; and He has deepened my appreciation for the Beatitudes and the love intrinsic to them. I frankly cannot imagine what my priesthood or apostolic zeal would be like without my little challenge. But I do know this: it would be less, much less.

• *"Offer it up."* One of the great mysteries of Christian life is that our suffering can, with Christ's suffering, help in the redemption of others. This is best explained in Jesus' final words on the Cross when He recited Psalm 22: "My God, my God, why have you forsaken me?" Jesus, here, was not referring only to the first line of that psalm, but rather to the psalm in its entirety. When one reads the psalm one notices a man who is going through a set of trials uncannily similar to Jesus' own sufferings on the Cross; but more importantly, one notices that the psalmist is not discouraged by the trials being suffered. He has a deep trust and confidence that God will use his sufferings not only for the good of the community around him, but also to bring all the nations to Himself in the future. Thus, when Jesus recited the words, "My God, my God, why have you forsaken me," He moved beyond the note of lamentation (in the first line) to a sublime confidence that the Father would effect universal salvation through His suffering. Recall for a moment what was said above about the Holy Eucharist, namely, that Jesus' Passion is His free gift of self, that is, His unconditional Love. When Jesus was dying on the Cross, He created a "gift of self," that is, an unconditional Love (as scapegoat, as paschal lamb, and as blood of the covenant) that He intended to give to the Father to shower down upon humanity so that all the nations might come into His kingdom of unconditional Love.

We can imitate Christ in our own limited ways by presenting our sufferings to the Father as a "gift of self" (love) for the Father to shower down upon humanity as a grace to strengthen and unify the mystical body of Christ. Every moment of suffering is a potential for a gift of love (grace) to be showered upon humanity in its need. All we need do to convert suffering into grace for the world is to *offer it up* to the Father as our gift of self.

When I was a child, I would complain to my mother about various things that had gone wrong at school, and she would say, very matter-of-factly, "Offer it up." My general reaction was, "I'm always offering it up, and no good seems to come from it." It only occurred to me years later that the offering was not intended to be a *direct* benefit to me, but rather a benefit for the world that would, in turn, be the efficacy of my life, which would, in turn, benefit me *indirectly* in the most important ways.

- "*I give up, Lord. You take care of it.*" Sometimes life gets out of control. No matter how hard we try to obviate freefall or to figure ourselves out, life's circumstances seem to get the better of us. It is at these moments that I recommend the above prayer, which I have put to great use throughout my life.

I recall my discovery of this prayer in Rome back in 1980. I had been sent to the Gregorian University to take all of my theology classes in Italian. I went to Italy two months early without any background in Italian to attain "fluency." I was reasonably confident after studying the language in Perugia for two months that I would be able to understand my classes. My first class on the first day was an exegesis class on the Gospel of Matthew taught by a Spanish professor who spoke Italian faster than the Italians (with a Spanish accent). I was not able to understand 25 percent of what he was saying and began to panic. What would I say to my Provincial? To my classmates? "Here I am, back in the United States. I couldn't understand anything and I flunked out." Needless to say, I began to feel considerable discomfort. Realizing that circumstances were quite out of my control, I muttered, "I give up, Lord. You take care of it!" When I said this it seemed like steam came out of my ears. A pressure was relieved by simply giving it over to the Lord, Who could providentially bring some good out of my predicament. As a matter of fact, He did. The moment this prayer enabled me to calm down, I became content with understanding partial sentences and concepts. I could then begin to make sense out of the general line of thought, which, in turn, built my confidence and thus enabled me to understand more. As the semester progressed, I began to understand far more of what the professor was saying and eventually made it to the final exam where the professor gave two or three choices of questions for various passages of Scripture. I was able to choose questions that pertained to the last parts of the course, thereby hiding my inadequate understanding of the first part. In the end, I did quite well. (Thank You, Lord!)

II. Prayers for Forgiveness

God's unconditional love makes the prayer of the publican continuously efficacious: "God, be merciful to me a sinner!" (Lk 18:13). As Jesus indicates, "this man went down to his house justified" (v. 14). Yet, there is even more to forgiveness in Christian life than the beauty of justification through God's unconditional Love. Two prayers may help to bring out these richer dimensions.

• *"Lord, I accept your forgiveness."* It is interesting how we can sometimes run from the incredibly liberating prayer of the publican because we think that God will hold back His forgiveness until we are "a little more deserving" or "a little less weak," or "a little more perfect."

When I was in the novitiate (the first stages of Jesuit formation) I slipped into the habit of believing that God had not quite forgiven me for my sins. Though I had heard the parable of the prodigal son and knew Jesus' address for the Father as *Abba*, though I was aware of His admonition to forgive seventy times seven times and tacitly aware of the implications of the Eucharist and the Passion (with respect to God's unconditional Love), I would come away from my prayer of repentance with the sneaking hunch that God was saying, "I wish I could forgive you, but unfortunately your repentance was not quite right and there's still too far to go before you're perfect enough to be forgiven." Since I did not want to be caught short, I would pray an alternative prayer: "Don't worry, God. I'll get it taken care of, and when everything is fine, then I'll be able to ask You for forgiveness, and then You will want to forgive me."

I had forgotten an important aspect about the spiritual life, namely, I *need* God—especially to turn my life around (*metanoia*). By putting so many limitations on God's love, mercy, and forgiveness, I had slipped into the worst of all possible spiritual attitudes (which is devilish, to say the least), for I had conditioned God's forgiveness on being "good enough," yet I could not be "good enough" without God's forgiveness and healing. The father of the prodigal son was standing outside my spiritual dome waving at me and trying to get my attention while I was busy turning him into a stoic ogre who would not want to give me his attention because I was not good enough.

Fortunately, my novice master recognized the insanity of my position and pointed to the conundrum, asking, "What does God have to gain by having you keep Him on the outside of your life—why in the world would God not want to get into your consciousness and help you clean up what you even perceive to be a mess?" It occurred to me that even if God were a pure pragmatist (which He is not), He would have nothing to gain by putting me into a position of zero progress and very probable regression. Since I was miserable, I readily assented to my novice master's point. He gave me the following advice, which I have maintained throughout my life: "When you ask for forgiveness, turn to God with the heart of a child who trusts unconditionally in his parents and say, 'I accept Your forgiveness.'" What a relief! Since God's love is unconditional, I can accept His forgiveness with the full knowledge that it is His intention to set me free. I have devised a three-step process for asking for forgiveness which accounts for this unconditional trust in *God's* unconditional Love:

First, affirm that God really is *Abba*, that God really possesses the unconditional Love of the prodigal son's father, that the divine Son really became incarnate and died in order to unconditionally give Himself away (in an act of unconditional Love), and that the Holy Spirit is really working to effect that unconditional Love within the world.

Second, affirm that God does want to forgive and heal you in order to work with you toward *metanoia*, and that God could have no other divergent attitude because it would lead to the demise of the whole human race.

Third, given this, when you ask for forgiveness, when you say, "Have mercy on me, Lord, for I am a sinful person," *accept* His forgiveness—accept it as the prodigal son returning to his father's house, accept it with the heart of a child who truly believes that his parents want to forgive him even after he has "gotten in trouble." Put on the mind and heart of Saint Peter at the Sea of Tiberias after Jesus'

Crucifixion when he hears John say, "It is the Lord" (Jn 21:7). After previously denying Jesus three times, Peter dives into the water and swims to shore, convinced that Jesus has but one thing in store for him: His healing and forgiving love. I took my novice master's advice and I put on the heart of a child, and when I address *Abba* I say, "Have mercy on me, Lord, for I am a sinful man. And I accept Your forgiveness and invite You into the depths of my soul so that You may call me to transformation."

- "*Make good come out of whatever harm I might have caused.*" The Lord's forgiving and healing love even extends to the people we might have harmed by our attitudes or actions. If the harm is intentional, we need to ask those who are harmed for forgiveness, for in this one act of humility we can redress the cycle of resentment begetting vengeance, vengeance begetting violence, and violence giving rise to further violence. We empower others to forgive us, and even if they should refuse, we are still the recipients of God's healing and forgiving love.

In the midst of trying to clear up harms or even possible harms, we often find ourselves powerless. Sometimes we do not recognize the depth of the hurt we might have caused; sometimes we are not even sure if we caused a harm; sometimes we only realize that we might have caused a harm hours after perpetrating a possible harm; sometimes we feel powerless when others cannot forgive us or talk to us. In all such cases there is a brief prayer that can prevent us from collapsing under the weight of our burden, a prayer that allows the grace of God (through the Holy Spirit) to work in the hearts of others, to effect eventual reconciliation and peace: "Lord, please make good come out of whatever harm I might have caused."

Many have been the times when I have found myself in such predicaments. Sometimes I am giving advice that I think will be quite fruitful, only to realize at three o'clock in the morning (when I wake up with startled lucidity) that I might have really "blown it." "Oh, no. That person might have taken the comment this way, or that other way, and may now be plunged into depression because of my idiocy . . . Arghh!" I think to myself, "He probably won't want a call at three o'clock in the morning to hear my attempt to straighten out the matter." At times like these, the above prayer is quite helpful. When I pray it (in confidence and trust), I sense the Holy Spirit working in the hearts of people I may have offended or harmed, and I sense a peace arising out of that confidence. I frequently find that my confidence is confirmed when the "victim" comes up to me a few days later and says, "Father Spitzer, when you said X, I really took it in the wrong way. I thought you meant Y, which really disturbed me; but the next day I got up and I got a different insight into what you were saying, and now I realize that you meant Z, which has been really helpful." As I listen to this great miracle of the Holy Spirit, I think to myself, "Whew!" I feel like Mario Andretti on a speedway after avoiding a potentially deadly crash by a split second. I have no question about who was doing the driving.

There are many other spontaneous prayers for healing and *metanoia* that I will try to cover in the chapters on contemplation (chapters 6 through 8).

III. Prayers Offering Forgiveness

• *"Lord, You are the just judge; You take care of it."* Jesus enjoins us to forgive one another from the heart, to forgive seventy times seven times, and to ask the Father to "forgive us our trespasses as we forgive those who trespass against us." It will probably come as no surprise that Jesus mentions this one prescription more often than any other commandment, injunction, or prescription in the New Testament. Why? Because violence begets violence, vengeance begets vengeance, resentment begets resentment, and the cycle will continue and grow so long as one of the offended parties does not let go. If one party does let go (forgives), the cycle frequently devolves, and forgiving eventually turns into forgetting.

One thing is clear: without forgiving, forgetting is impossible, indeed, the opposite occurs. The memory of an offense seems to mushroom in its proportions and emotional discharge. When I am in a "nonforgiving mood," I tend to exaggerate all the bad features of a memory, omit all the good features of the perpetrator, and attempt to construct a scenario whereby the demon-other has perpetrated the unforgivable—then I get *good* and mad. Without forgiveness, the reliving of a scenario seems to get worse with every self-retelling. The above prayer has helped me immensely in this regard: "Lord, You are the just Judge; You take care of it."

I remember the time I discovered this prayer. I had written a philosophical paper and a colleague criticized it behind my back. When I had publicly read the paper, I had given ample opportunity for questions and had even submitted the paper to selected individuals before reading it. This particular colleague said nothing. But a few days later, he was not only critical of the paper, but also of me. When someone called this to my attention, I was quite angry. Even after I had addressed the criticism in writing, I felt no relief. In fact, my anger began to grow. Every time I opened my breviary, this person's face suddenly appeared. Instead of taking the hint from God, I chose to stew in my anger. Finally, it occurred to me that this was only hurting *me*, and, furthermore, it might cause me to say something I would regret; so I had to face it.

I first tried to face it on my own; "Okay . . . now I'm going to stop thinking about this and I'm going to forgive this person from the heart"; but every time I tried the "solo method" I found myself having about one-half second of peace followed by an intense burst of anger. I was quite helpless. Finally, it occurred to me—why not let God help? So I said, "Okay, Lord, you're the just Judge. You can see into the hearts of every human being. You understand our history and our failings. You can effect reconciliation where mere mortals cannot. Okay, You take care of him; in fact, You take care of the whole situation, please." An unbelievable peace began to come over me. By putting this person (and the past situation) into God's hands, I allowed the Holy Spirit to work His reconciling love through His infinite providence in my heart. In letting go (into *God's* hands), I was eventually able to forget; and, in the forgetting, I was able not only to find peace, but also to even smile at and acknowledge the person who had offended me. This is a powerful prayer, and I have used it often. The immense reconciling love of the Holy Spirit cannot be underestimated in its power to transform and bring peace. This leads to the next prayer.

• *Prayer for Enemies.* Jesus admonishes us to "love your enemies, do good to those who hate you, bless those who curse you, pray for those who abuse you" (Lk 6:27–28). Paul does the same by saying, "If your enemy is hungry, feed him; if he is thirsty, give him drink" (Rom 12:20). In both my life and leadership positions I have found no greater advice. What at first appeared to be virtually impossible (and purely ironical), I have found to be not only possible, but utterly efficacious and transformative. Throughout my career, I have found myself in conflict with people (sometimes justifiably, sometimes not). I have seen how these conflicts can intensify in emotion when people continue to think the worst about one another. These emotions can become so heightened that there seems to be no way of reconciling (or even communicating) with the parties in conflict.

When this occurs, I begin my campaign to pray for those who feel extremely angered by me or who may be trying to harm me. I ask at least three or four times a day that the Lord enter into their hearts, show them His love, and bring them to Himself. The response is absolutely remarkable—a great majority of the time, the person for whom I am praying will show a marked decrease in hostility within days. Sometimes the person displays an openness to compromise and even manifest understanding and compassion for both me and my position. This connection between prayer and "completely unexpected results" is so highly correlative, I recommend that people practice it not only to effect reconciliation, but also to see firsthand the power of prayer! Again, the power of the Holy Spirit to work through the hearts of intrinsically dignified human beings and to draw them toward the love for which they were created cannot be underestimated.

IV. "Thy Will Be Done"

Without a doubt, the most important prayer of all is "Thy will be done." Jesus teaches us this prayer in the Our Father (see Mt 6:9–15) and uses it Himself at the agony in the garden (see Mt 26:39–44). Since that time, it has become a centerpiece of Christian spiritual life. It can be used in times of fear, temptation, anger, trial; indeed, it may be substituted for all of the prayers given above. If you cannot remember any other prayer, default to this one.

Why? Because the will of God is optimally loving, optimally good, optimally just, and optimally salvific; and when the will of God is working through you, you become an instrument of His optimally loving, good, just, and salvific will in the world; you become the agent of a legacy that will last into eternity, an agent for the kingdom of God manifest on earth and perpetuated for eternity. There could be no more worthy purpose for living than this. That is why this prayer can make good come out of our harms, can make good come out of our trials, can calm us in the heat of anger, can help us in times of temptation, and can bring salvation out of every seemingly negative course of events. If we give our problems over to God by praying, "Thy will be done," He will bring good for us, others, the community, the culture, and His kingdom out of the most bizarre, tragic, desolate, angering, hurtful, fearful, tempting, and confusing dimensions of our lives. In that efficacious will, there is peace, a peace beyond all understanding (see Phil 4:7). I say this prayer at least twenty-five times a day, and I find the all-loving will of God and the immense providence of the Holy Spirit to be unbelievably efficacious and transformative.

There is only one thing to remember: one cannot have the wrong attitude about God or His will. If we forget that God is *Abba*, the father of the prodigal son, the Father of Jesus the Beloved One, Unconditional Love itself, and consequently we start attributing antithetical qualities to Him, such as stoic indifference to us, competition with us, getting even with us for past offenses, adolescent anger and retribution, lack of forgiveness and mercy, unkindness, boastfulness, or any other attribute contrary to the "Hymn to Love" in First Corinthians 13, then the will of God will not seem optimally loving, good, just, and salvific, but rather as a sword of Damocles ready to drop on our heads in some capricious fashion. When we believe that God's will is harmful or capricious, we cannot bring ourselves to ask for it; instead, we run for cover. We deprive ourselves of the most powerful, spontaneous prayer the Lord has given us.

I had an experience of this in my first month at the Jesuit novitiate. We were given the prayer of Saint Ignatius to say each night at our final prayers: "Take, Lord, receive all my liberty, my memory, my understanding, and my entire will. Whatsoever I have or hold, You have given to me. I give it all back to You. Dispose of it wholly according to Your will. Give me only Your love and Your grace, and that's enough for me, and I ask for nothing more." As can be seen, this is an enlarged and eloquent way of saying, "Thy will be done."

Unfortunately, when I first came to the novitiate I had not appropriated (in either my mind or heart) the unconditional love, goodness, justice, and salvation intrinsic to the will of God. As a result, I prayed this prayer in what now appears to me to be an incredibly humorous (but at the time fearful and painstaking) way. I began by saying, "T-t-take, L-Lord, receive all my liberty (but I really like my liberty, so don't destroy it if I give it to You; on second thought, I'll take it back for safekeeping); m-m-my memory (but You gave me a good memory, and I really need it, and I really use it, so please don't destroy it if I give it to You; on second thought, I'll take it back for safekeeping); m-m-my u-understanding (but You gave me a fine intellect and I really use it, so please don't destroy it if I give it to You—I think I'll take it back for safekeeping. . . .) Whew! I made it through that prayer and I'm still intact." This clearly was not the intention of Saint Ignatius, who probably would have been mystified by the sheer panic I was experiencing in giving myself over to God's will.

This prayer takes on a completely opposite significance when one remembers that God's will is to bring optimal love, goodness, justice, and salvation out of every fiber of our being and every aspect of our actions. But *we need to ask for this* because He has created us with a freedom that can actually ignore, hide from, or even refuse His absolutely positive and unconditionally loving intent. When we remember this intent, the prayer of Saint Ignatius presents to God our freedom to be used for His optimally loving, good, just, and salvific purposes. We present Him too with our memory and our intellect and our entire will for these eternally perduring purposes, which transforms our lives into something so efficacious that its dimension can only be grasped through the mind of God after our passing.

Of course, one need not pray the whole prayer of Saint Ignatius throughout the busyness of our daily lives. It is sufficient to simply say, "Thy will be done"—whenever the need arises. In my life, the need arises frequently.

Chapter Three

Third Pillar: The Beatitudes

Introduction

If we are to be contemplatives *in action*, then we will have to take the fruit of our prayer (the fruit of Christ's teaching that has *love* as its center) into our lives (family, organization, community, church). Likewise, we must take the lessons learned through human discourse and leadership back into our prayer. I believe that this cycle lies behind Jesus' connection of His first two commandments (love of God with one's whole being and love of neighbor as oneself).

When Jesus elevated love (*agape*) to the highest of all commandments (for the first time in the history of religions), He also placed the love of God and neighbor in a complementary relationship. He took two distinct commands from two books of the Old Testament Torah (Deut 6:5 and Lev 19:18, respectively) and synthesized them as first and second commandments. In so doing, He elevated the love of neighbor (which had hitherto been viewed as a moderately heavy commandment) to the second heaviest of all commandments and implied that it flows out of and complements the love of God. Thus, Jesus saw the love of God flowing into and expanding the love of neighbor while the love of neighbor flowed back into and expanded the love of God. The two are in a relationship like an ever-widening spiral.

If we are to appreciate the significance of this moral revolution, we will want to understand what Jesus meant by "love." This is perhaps best understood through the Beatitudes, which summarize His moral and spiritual teachings while providing a conduit between the love of God and the love of neighbor (the contemplative life and the active life). Before proceeding to the Beatitudes (the conditions, habits, and fruits of love), it may be helpful to provide a definition that probes the nature of love (*agape*) according to Jesus.

Agape may be defined as the kind of love that does not require feelings of affection (in Greek, *storgê*), the mutuality of friendship (being cared for, committed to, complemented by, and at home with the other—in Greek, *philia*), or romantic or libidinal feelings (in Greek, *eros*). Indeed, *agape* does not require any feeling, reward, or return (mutuality) whatsoever. It is love that arises out of an empathetic recognition of and connection to the unique, *intrinsic dignity*, goodness, and mystery of the other.

The unique, intrinsic dignity of the other may be captured in a benevolent glance, a conversation, or a sense of the other's unique presence. Once captured, it provokes an awareness of the *intrinsic* value, worth, or goodness of the other, and this, in its turn, provokes a desire to help, protect, and enhance this intrinsically valuable, good, mysterious other. An empathetic connection (a unity) then forms, whereby doing the good for that unique other is just as easy, if not easier, than doing the good for oneself.

The empathy that leads to *agape* cannot occur if we are fixated on the bad news in the other (that is, what is irritating, weak, stupid, unkind, etc.). Unfortunately, this bad news is frequently easier to see (and to become fixated on) than the good news in the other. But it is virtually impossible to look for the bad news when you are looking for the good news, and that good news is the path to empathy, and that empathy is the path to *agape*, and that *agape* is the path to God.

The Beatitudes express the conditions, habits, and fruits of *agape*. In order to explain them within the life of prayer, it may do well to begin with a contemporary English translation and then proceed to an interpretation of them (as might have been understood by Jesus' contemporaries).

> How blessed are the poor in spirit, for theirs is the kingdom of heaven.
> Blessed are the sorrowing, they shall be consoled.
> Blessed are the meek, they shall inherit the land.
> Blessed are those who hunger and thirst for righteousness, they shall have their fill.
> Blessed are the merciful, mercy shall be theirs.
> Blessed are the pure of heart, they shall see God.
> Blessed are the peacemakers, they shall be called children of God.
> Blessed are those persecuted for righteousness' sake, the kingdom of God is theirs.
> Blessed are you when men insult you and hate you and utter every kind of slander falsely because of me. Rejoice and be glad, for your reward in heaven will be great. (Mt 5:3–12)

These concepts may be roughly interpreted in contemporary terms as follows:

Blessed are the humble-hearted.

Blessed are the sorrowing.

Blessed are the gentle-hearted.

Blessed are those who hunger and thirst for the will of God.

Blessed are the forgiving and the merciful.

Blessed are the pure of heart (interior motives).

Blessed are the peacemakers and reconcilers.

Blessed are those persecuted for the will of God.

Blessed are you when men insult you and hate you. . . .

A quick overview will show that six of the Beatitudes describe fundamental interior attitudes while three of them describe conditions of life that God will alleviate, heal, and sanctify in the kingdom of heaven (the sorrowing, the persecuted for holiness' sake, and "you" when you are persecuted for the kingdom). Thus, the six central virtues describing Jesus' view of love (*agape*) are (1) humble-heartedness, (2) gentleheartedness, (3) an intense desire for the will of God, (4) forgiveness and mercy, (5) purity of heart, and (6) peacemaking and reconciling.

I. Blessed Are the Humble-Hearted (the Poor in Spirit)

Humble-heartedness is the most fundamental interior disposition. It is constituted by two major elements: (1) placing the needs of others before our own, and (2) knowing our proper place in the grand scheme of things.

1. *Placing the needs of others before our own.* As noted in chapter 1, section IV, everyone must choose between a Level 1–2 identity (focusing on possession, pleasure, ego-gratification, and comparative advantage) and a Level 3–4

identity (focusing on making an optimal positive difference with one's life through contribution, love, and faith).

A Level 2 purpose tries to shift the locus of control from the outer world to the inner world. Hence, it seeks status, admiration, winning, control, and power, which all entail comparisons—"Who has got more status? Who has got less status?" etc. Conversely, Level 3 purpose moves in the opposite direction. It seeks to invest life, talent, and energy in making a positive difference to somebody or something beyond the self. It finds happiness and fulfillment, therefore, in making the world a better place for others.

These two desires are not incompatible, for when Level 2 serves Level 3 (i.e., Level 2 is the *means* and Level 3 is the *end*), Level 2 is both healthy and efficacious. However, when Level 2 becomes *an end in itself*, it tends to cancel out Level 3 (because Level 2 and Level 3 cannot both be *ends* at the same time). This Level 2 purpose not only causes a lack of contribution to the world (the common good), but also emptiness, jealousy, fear of failure, ego-sensitivity, blame, contempt, resentment, self-pity, and other negative emotions (see the Epilogue to this book). Inasmuch as a Level 3 identity (which is essential to humble-heartedness) alleviates these negative emotions and enables us to make a positive difference with our lives, it not only conforms to God's will, but also brings happiness. Thus, you may want to take literally Jesus' first Beatitude: "Blessed [happy] are the poor in spirit [the humble-hearted], for theirs is the kingdom of heaven."

How might we best initiate this lifelong process of looking for the contributive before the comparative? I recommend that you buy a quality journal and write down all the ways in which you can make an optimal positive difference (with *your* time, talent, energy, and creativity) to the various individuals and groups who touch your life. Start with the most intimate and work your way out to more general groups: "How can I make an optimal positive difference to my family members, and to my family as a whole? How can I make an optimal positive difference to my friends? To my church? To the kingdom of God? To God? How can I make an optimal positive difference to my organization, to my co-workers, my colleagues, my employees? How can I make an optimal positive difference to my community, community center, civic boards? To my cultural boards, culture, and society?" Some of these categories may not be meaningful to your life—simply pick the ones that are relevant. Dedicate two or three hours on a Saturday and begin to reflect on this most important matter in a deliberate yet serendipitous way.

When you have completed your first draft of this list (assume that there will be other drafts as you move through the stages of life), put down, at the bottom of the page(s), "For this I came." This will definitively associate your concrete, contributive goals with your purpose in life. Use this list as a basis for your reflection and Examen (see chapter 8, section II) at least once a week for the next year. Your contributive purpose will *slowly* become your *subconscious* purpose and then *slowly* become your heart's desire.

Two additional points must be made in this regard. First, contributive identity can have two forms: "doing" and "being with." "Doing" is fairly simple to understand in this culture. It includes any activity that enhances the well-being of another. It could be writing a book, giving a person a ride to work, inventing a new system, teaching a catechism class, etc. In our culture, "being with" is more difficult to see, and even more difficult to value; but many times it can be of far greater importance. It might include playing "Crazy 8s" with nieces, listening to an older person tell you about her struggles, giving a friend time (because he needs that more than some good, concise advice), or spending more time with a spouse or children. The important thing to remember is that one can make as much of a positive difference to other persons by simply being present, giving time, listening, and being attentive, as one can by doing something for them.

When I was in the novitiate, my Latin instructor was a rather delightful ninety-year-old priest. One day, I was passing by the television room where the seminarians and priests lived and noticed him watching a Notre Dame game all by himself. I popped in to watch the last five minutes of the game with him. We didn't say a word to each other during the game, but only snorted, cheered, or laughed in what seemed to be our own private worlds. After the game was over (Notre Dame won), I got up to leave. He pushed himself out of his chair and said to me, "Thank you, brother. Watching the game with you made all the difference." It immediately occurred to me how powerful mere presence is in "making a positive difference" to the world. It can even be presence in something as intrinsically delightful as a winning Notre Dame game.

Second, we must be very wary of Level 2 propensities engulfing and even taking over our Level 3 identities. The most common occurrence of this in my life is when I look at someone who is a very effective and loving minister in the Lord's service and think to myself, "Hmm . . . I think I'm doing more good than he is" (that is, "I'm still okay"). A contemptuous variant of this is "I'm doing more good than you are—I don't know how you can live with so few Level 3 accomplishments. But I guess you're okay with your life."

As may now be evident, this takes all the wind out of my Level 3 sails, for I am no longer doing the contributive for the sake of others, but only for the sake of being *better than* others or aggrandizing my list of accomplishments. Even if I never tell anyone about my aggrandized list of accomplishments (but only admire it for myself three times per day), I may find myself still living for Level 2 instead of Level 3, and therefore of canceling out my desire for Level 3. I have been there, done that—many times.

The only way to prevent these sneaky Level 2 desires from reemerging is to keep our eyes focused on the other to whom we are making a positive difference. This is not as easy a task as might at first be thought, because the ego-comparative identity is both a default, a delight, and a powerful force. In my life I have been able to keep my eye "on the other whom I am serving" only through the grace of God. The prayer "Thy will be done"; the Eucharist, which transforms me; the Holy Spirit, Who guides me; and the contemplative life, which deepens me—these are the tools I have in order to combat what otherwise would assail and overtake me. "But thanks be to God, who gives us the victory through our Lord Jesus Christ" (1 Cor 15:57). This brings us to the second major element in humble-heartedness.

2. *Knowing our proper place in the grand scheme of things.* Knowing my proper place entails replacing myself (as the center of my interior universe) with God, Who properly belongs there, and then finding a *coequal* place around the center with my neighbors (who are the *image* of God).

I am but one coequal member of that invaluably dignified community. My purpose in life is to enhance and be co-responsible for whatever part of the community that God might want me to help.

We can best love our neighbor (that is, see the dignity of our neighbor, appreciate and help our neighbor, and be the most effective disciples of Christ) when we are free from having to be the center of our and other people's universes. Being God for ourselves and others is a most difficult task. It requires enormous amounts of energy. It seems as though there is virtually no time to attend to the concerns of neighbor, community, and culture when one is preoccupied with being the best human on the block, the Messiah, or even God. If one wants subservient respect from others (rather than loving respect), one will have little time to build up the common good and the kingdom of God, because one will have to spend the bulk of one's time cultivating the tools and attitudes of domination. True freedom (that is, having the time and energy to do what really matters) can be actualized through simply knowing who one is and "is meant to be."

Unfortunately, it is not that simple. Every time I discover a new talent, or master a new academic area, or accomplish something new, or attain to a higher status, I seem to go through the same old cycle of troubles. First, I try to define my life in terms of the particular success (for example, a new book, a new institute, a success for the university, and so forth). This imparts not only a feeling of accomplishment, but also a feeling of comparative advantage (superiority) and even a sense of world-changing (quasi-messianic) dignity. I move from "the world being better off for my having lived," to "I am an indispensable and central part of my and others' universes." When people respect me for my accomplishments, I begin to think, "I'm a little bit better than other people. They ought to be a little bit more subservient (and even beholden) to me for deigning to be in their presence."

This leads to a second part of the cycle, namely, erratic emotions arising out of jealousy, fear of failure, suspicion of others, inferiority, superiority, self-pity, blaming others for everything that goes wrong, exaggerating my strengths, dissatisfaction with my progress in life, ego-sensitivity, inability to fail or be wrong, and resentment for insignificant mistakes and oversights (see the Epilogue). My easily perceptible egoism and my erratic emotions cause people (even the most sympathetic ones) to avoid me and even disrespect me. Since I desire their respect more than anything, my life suffers reversals.

This results in a third phase, namely, choice. I can either try to move into higher gear to obtain the respect lost in the previous phase or I can decide to be humble as Christ was humble. If I take the first route, I perpetuate the cycle once again, exhaust myself even more, find myself still more disappointed with life, and find myself closer to the edge and even more hyperactive.

But there is a way out. For me, it begins with prayer, prayer that might be as simple as reading my breviary or saying the Rosary. Prayer, by its very nature, has a way of reestablishing my proper place. I have frequently had the experience after a bout of real arrogance (and even self-idolatry) of opening my breviary and finding myself sliding back toward my proper place as God slides into His central place. As I read the second psalm and then the third psalm, and then the reading, and then the responsory, things become "more normal" and a calm begins to ensue. I can always tell when God is moving toward the center of the universe again because I enjoy—simply enjoy—praising Him. In a way, starting the prayer lets God slide into the center, and as He slides into the center, I delight in praising Him more and more, and in that delight, the calm of humble-heartedness begins. This moment in prayer, this reason for the contemplative life, this nexus of contemplation and action frees me to be a neighbor among many other neighbors, and allows me to be unconditionally loved by God (Who is also unconditionally loving others), and to be content with imitating Him in that love. Through prayer, I am free enough (humble-hearted enough) to appreciate the invaluable goodness of my neighbor, love my neighbor, accept my neighbor's love, and be content to serve my Lord and His kingdom with a joyful and eager heart.

This first Beatitude reveals the necessity for the contemplative life, for without that life, humble-heartedness and all its freedoms and loves would be (at least for me) impossible. I cannot bring myself to humble-heartedness, and even if I could, the very attempt to bring *myself* there would jerk me out of my proper place into some other messianic realm over which I have no control. Contemplation's beauty resides in its being the vehicle for God to move our hearts toward our proper place (in freedom and love; see chapters 6–8).

II. Blessed Are the Gentle-Hearted (Meek)

Gentle-heartedness follows from humble-heartedness. When I know my proper place, and am therefore free to appreciate and affirm the invaluable goodness of my neighbor, I can afford to be gentle. By "gentle," here, I do not mean the gentility of a superior patting, as it were, an inferior on the head, but rather a fundamental recognition of the depth, uniqueness, and transcendentality of another person, emanating from his eyes, voice, and mere presence. This vision of the other engenders a profound insight into my coequality with him, which in turn engenders a deep insight into my co-responsibility with him for the common good and the good of God's kingdom. I feel as though I am on the same team with him in manifesting the kingdom of God, that we have a common purpose, and that no one needs to be superior or inferior in that project. All that is required is that each person's functional specialty be respected and honored.

I can always tell when things are going well on the "gentle-heartedness front," because I can take delight in people without diminishing them in relationship to me. I can enjoy their insight, love, zeal for the kingdom, courage, wisdom, and faith as a grace, as God speaking to me through them. I can also enjoy them as intrinsically delightful, uniquely invaluable "little eternities" beloved by God.

As with humble-heartedness, gentle-heartedness begins with prayer. It is in part dependent upon humble-heartedness, but also occupies its own dimension of prayer. As I open my breviary and pray the Psalms, I find myself gradually becoming more comforted by the love of God. As I take delight in God, I become more aware of His deeper delight in me. I am convinced that this emotional bond of friendship is not self-induced, for it is not like reading poetry or good literature. It is God's grace working through psalms that may not be the best poetry or may not have the most modern images, but nevertheless express praise with the heart of a child filled with wonder. There is something about the faith of the psalmist, when set within the context of the love of

Christ and the Spirit speaking with ineffable groanings, which enflames my heart with desire for the Lord, Who, in turn, infuses me with a sense of being beloved. When I am beloved by such a Lord, it is hard for me not to see the belovedness of others, and it is this vision of belovedness that opens the door to "delighting in them as coequals and coheirs in the mission of Christ and the kingdom of God." This is the source of the genuine gentle-heartedness that I believe Jesus was trying to incite in the Beatitudes. When it is combined with humble-heartedness (i.e., God and us in our proper places), it leads almost inevitably to love of neighbor.

Before proceeding to the third attitude, it might be helpful to look at the first two Beatitudes from the perspective of leadership. Some leaders may be thinking to themselves, "I can't afford to be humble-hearted and gentle-hearted. It's a tough world out there, and people are trying to take advantage of me and my company. I have to be a tough negotiator, even tougher with my competitors, and driven toward a goal. If I am not, I abdicate my responsibility to the shareholders of this company. Yet, I am a good Christian, and so I would like to know my place and treat others with the coequal respect they deserve. I know . . . I'll be humble-hearted and gentle-hearted in my family, community, and faith life, but will revert to contrary tendencies in the workplace. I don't want a bifurcated personality, but I don't see any other way around it."

This attitude has certainly gone through my mind on more than one occasion. I have felt very protective of Gonzaga's competitive position and the stakeholders (the faculty, staff, students, alumni, parents, community members, etc.), who are dependent on a strong and thriving institution. So it has occurred to me that it would be perfectly appropriate to do some crushing and smashing as might be needed in that protective service. However, as will be seen, this particular view of protectiveness is illusory.

Let us return to our definitions for a moment. Recall that humble-heartedness is knowing my place relative to God and others, and that gentle-heartedness is seeing the coequal *dignity* of others in their "belovedness by God" and in their invaluable eternal soul. There is nothing in these definitions about having to be a wimp or a milquetoast. Frankly, Jesus was neither of these. He was rather firm with the scribes and Pharisees, a rather tough negotiator, very protective of not only His disciples, but of all those who were in need of help and justification (*His* stakeholders, so to speak). Yet Jesus, acutely aware of His incredibly special relationship with *Abba*, His mission of bringing no less than the kingdom of God to earth, and of being the apocalyptic Son of Man (the eschatological Judge), was consummately gentle-hearted. He wanted to make all of us His brothers, particularly those who were poor and marginalized, even those who fell outside the law. Jesus enjoyed being with them, not as superior to inferior, but as beloved to beloved, intensely desiring to raise up the eternal, invaluable, unique spirit within every human being in every state of life. Can that attitude be harmful to leadership?

I would definitively say no. Leadership is enhanced by the humble-heartedness that knows one's place. When one tries to be messiah (instead of mere leader), people are neither pleased nor fooled. A false messiah is a flash in the pan. Such people tend to leave small, short-lived legacies with thousands of resentments and people problems in their wake. In contrast to this, those who have a sense of their co-responsibility with others in building up the kingdom of *God* tend to leave profound, long-lasting legacies filled with an ethos of respect and even noble virtue. Those who try to be messianic find themselves scorned, while those who manifest the highest moments of humble, vision-driven leadership find themselves heroes. Those who exalt themselves will be humbled, and those who humble themselves will be exalted. The literature of leadership is replete with examples of military, business, civic, religious, educational, and cultural leaders who, in mere brief moments of humility, left legacies for generations. It is also replete with examples of the opposite—the dashed plans of pride coming before the fall. Today's leaders would be well served to live by Jesus' standard, and if prayer is the one failsafe means to get there, then we would be well served to reserve fifteen minutes a day to immerse ourselves in a breviary, a Rosary, a *Magnificat*, and, if time permits, to receive the Holy Eucharist. This will enable us to attain for our stakeholders what we cannot give by ourselves.

The same holds true for gentle-heartedness. Leaders who see the intrinsic dignity of others (who see the "who" alongside the "what") are capable of empathy. As such, they will never undervalue their co-workers, and, like good mentors, will see more in their co-workers than their co-workers can see in themselves. Such individuals inspire others. They don't have to *sell* the vision of the organization because others believe in them, sense their charisma, and trust in their humility and respectfulness. Inspirational leaders cannot help themselves. They tend to make organizations great by the addictiveness of their personality, the belief in their vision, and the dignity they accord to others. One thing is certain: in the end, inspirational leaders must be gentle-hearted. Arrogance, superiority, and contempt do not inspire; they only lead to resentment, pushback, defensiveness, and unpleasant politics. This is how normal people react to domination and self-aggrandizement. Again, today's leaders would be well served to follow the standard of Christ rather than flee from it, for in gentle-heartedness and humble-heartedness there is the fabric of the collective human spirit inspired to a vision beyond itself. What more could any leader want?

III. Blessed Are Those Who Hunger and Thirst for the Will of God (Holiness)

Intensely desiring the will of God also follows from humble-heartedness. When one realizes God's place and, through prayer, realizes the immensity, the beauty, and the love of God, one cannot help but want what God wants. But it is not simply the nobility, the beauty, the eternity, and the goodness of God's *mission* that makes God's will attractive; it is also the lovability of God Himself.

When I am celebrating Mass or praying the breviary or Rosary, I am frequently struck by how much God loves not only me, but the people around me. Thanks to the Holy Spirit, this awareness is as poignant as a friend saying, "I just love that person." I can almost sense God's concern and tenderness for the people around me as I pray Psalm 8:

> O Lord, our Lord,
> how majestic is your name in all the earth!
> You whose glory above the heavens is chanted
>   by the mouth of babies and infants,
> you have founded a bulwark . . .

When I look at your heavens, the work of your fingers,
> the moon and the stars which you have established;
what is man that you are mindful of him,
> and the son of man that you care for him?
Yet you have made him little less than the angels,
> and you have crowned him with glory and honor.
You have given him dominion over the works of your hands;
> you have put all things under his feet. (Ps 8:1–6)

As I marvel at the love God has for us, the glory with which He has crowned us, as I sense His deep concern and tenderness for me and the people around me, as I consider the goodness, lovability, eternity, and nobility of His will, I cannot help but desire it for love of Him and His mission. Saint Ignatius points out that God works through desire, and in prayer God enflames our desire for His love and His will. It is almost irresistible; and when I follow my heart's desire, I find myself not only caught up in the beauty of His spirit and mission, but also blessed—happy—indeed (just as Jesus promised).

IV. Blessed Are the Forgiving and Merciful

As discussed in chapter 2, forgiveness is one of Jesus' key concerns in the moral life. It is the condition necessary for love to prevail. As we saw earlier, vengeance begets vengeance and violence begets violence, and the only thing that will interrupt these destructive (anti-loving) cycles is forgiveness (the act of letting go so that forgetting can eventually occur). Forgiveness, then, is the spiritual power to start over again, the condition necessary for healing. It is therefore the condition necessary for the human community to progress in faith, hope, and love.

Forgiveness is also a primary manifestation of compassion and love, for it is truly a gift of self. Recall that we need to forgive when someone has truly done us an injustice. In a way, we own the degradation and the pain of that injustice; it is like a debt that we can hold onto forever (even though the other person might not acknowledge it or intend to rectify it). When we forgive, we let the debt go, and it is like giving away a prized possession, or, better, an important part of ourselves. When we do this it truly manifests the highest degree of generosity for the good of the *other* and even the human community. This is love.

Love (like all acts of self-gift and compassion) civilizes us. It puts the other ahead of us. It enables us to become *a* part of the human community (instead of *the* part or *the central* part of the human community). In so doing, it acknowledges the reality of ourselves before God, which, in its turn, grants us a freedom to live for the will and kingdom of God. This freedom brings peace, joy, transformation, and efficacy in life.

Forgiveness is very difficult to accomplish on our own. But it can be done through our faith: "With men this is impossible, but with God all things are possible" (Mt 19:26). The spontaneous prayer, "Lord, You are the just Judge; You take care of it" is probably the best spontaneous prayer I have had the opportunity to use in this regard. By itself, this prayer can bestow great freedom and grace, but its effects are remarkably enhanced through an increase in the other four pillars. Thus, the Holy Eucharist, the practice of the other Beatitudes, the Holy Spirit, and the contemplative life give this little prayer a vast power of detachment, freedom, and love that surpasses anything I might be able to do on my own. The contemplative life is particularly important in this regard.

I was once asked by a student at Georgetown University why he should "bother" with building a contemplative life if he was faithful to the other four pillars (the Eucharist, spontaneous prayer, the Beatitudes, and the Holy Spirit). He was a very busy and successful student and was having difficulty seeing "the practicality" of using his precious time for the more passive pursuits of contemplation when he could be "chalking up" more achievements for the present and future kingdom of God. I indicated to him that the need for contemplation was not merely a matter of quantity, but *quality*—quality of life, quality of relationships, and quality of apostolic actions. This appealed to his very practical mentality because he could see "value added" in his actions. Throughout his time at Georgetown he began to discover that contemplation brought peace (in times of tribulation), joy (reveling in the kingdom of God), and hope and trust (in God's presence, eternal salvation, and even victory in human history), which, in their turn, led to an ability to "hand things over to God," a transformation of desire (from attachment to worldly desires, to attachment to the kingdom and the will of God as primary desires), and, finally, the ability to love. I spoke with this same student about two years ago. He has become a priest and told me that he was quite grateful to me for this simple truth about contemplation. I must admit that he was an "easy sell," but many of us, including myself, are not. I was similar to him as a young man in my desire to "chalk up achievements for the kingdom." Unfortunately, I had to learn the value of contemplation through the school of "hard knocks" and "fits and starts." I believe it is one of the top ten discoveries of my life, for once discovered and acted upon, it provided a vehicle for God to bring enormous freedom and transformation amidst peace, joy, trust, and hope. This is the way God cultivates the heart for love. I will give a more detailed explanation of these matters in chapters 6–8 (on the contemplative life).

Now, back to forgiveness and mercy. "Mercy" has a broader meaning than "forgiveness." It also entails what are called the "corporal works of mercy" (that is, assistance for the poor and the needy, both temporally and spiritually). But "mercy" here is not restricted to *works* (behaviors) of mercy; it is also concerned with the *heart* of mercy, which leads to works. As by now might be apparent, Jesus has oriented the Beatitudes (and, quite frankly, His entire teaching) toward the heart (one's fundamental interior disposition toward love). The merciful heart keeps an eye out for those in need. It is sensitive to those who are lonely, helpless, deprived, disadvantaged, ignored, and pushed to the periphery. And it moves one to respond to these needs with available (and even sacrificial) time, resources, and psychic energy.

I cannot exaggerate how important a merciful heart is to Jesus—that is, a heart that responds to spiritual and temporal need with compassion, care, and love. Two of the few times that Jesus uses the language of eternal judgment occur within parables about people who do not have a heart of mercy: (1) the parable of Lazarus and the rich man (see Lk 16:19–31), where the hardening of the rich man's heart separates him from Abraham and the kingdom of heaven, and (2) the parable of the sheep and the goats (Mt 25:31–46), where the goats seem incapable of responding to the hungry, thirsty, lonely, naked, sick, and imprisoned, and so find themselves alienated from God. Why would Jesus use this infrequent and threatening mode of expression in these contexts? Because He is worried—*very* worried that if people do not open their hearts to the needy, they will not open their hearts to anyone; and if they do not open their hearts to anyone, they will not open their hearts to God; and if they do not open their hearts to God, then they will not accept His compassion and love. Jesus uses threatening language to shake us out of possible complacency, to make us place "the cultivation of a heart of mercy"—a heart responding to temporal and spiritual need—at the top of our "To Do" list. If we do cultivate this heart—this heart like Jesus'—we will never regret it. It will be the opening to not only the love of neighbor, but the love of God, and this will be our true joy.

Recall from the explanation of "blessed are the poor in spirit [humble-hearted]" (section I) that the cultivation of our hearts begins with selecting a Level 3/Level 4 identity or purpose in life. It begins not with being perfect (indeed, after a lifetime one is still in desperate need of God's grace to achieve perfection in love), but rather with choosing (even if only intellectually) a purpose in life that seeks to optimize the positive difference we can make with our time, talent, and energy. This seeking of the contributive (above the comparative) allows God to work His wonders of gradually deepening conversion within our hearts.

However, there is always a danger that our Level 2 desires will reassume a dominant role amidst our choice of Level 3/ Level 4 identity (for example, "I'm doing more good than you are—I'm the social hero; I'm the best. I'm almost a messiah"). So long as we can keep that Level 2 dominance at bay by calling on the help and mercy of God, God can work His wonders in our souls to remove the layers of hardness, which seem to exist in us all.

The choice of a Level 3/Level 4 identity combined with the gentle love of the Spirit awakens us, and we become gradually more *aware* of the temporal needs of others around us (e.g., those who are lonely, marginalized, poor, homeless, sick, suffering from dementia, oppressed by individuals, or oppressed by governments) and of the spiritual needs of others around us (e.g., those who are unacquainted with the loving God, who have no sense of hope, who believe that life is absurd, who have made recourse to self-sufficiency instead of love, to cynicism instead of trust, or to material dignity instead of transcendental dignity). The more we engage our awareness (by responding to the needs of others), the more sensitized we become to these temporal and spiritual needs; and the more sensitized we become, the more we will want to engage them. The cycle will continue so long as we call upon the Lord's help and mercy to keep our Level 2 desires in their proper place.

Two caveats should be mentioned here. First, different people are better equipped to respond to different needs. Some people are well equipped to go to the missions; some others to work in the homeless shelters; others to work with troubled teenagers; others to work with the elderly. Some are meant to be educators; some to be spiritual directors; others to be agents of change in culture; and others to be a prophetic voice. Some are best equipped to write; some to speak; and some to be hands-on. Some to work with older people; some to work with younger people; and some to work with the middle-aged. Whatever the case, we must always bear in mind the words of Saint Paul in his First Letter to the Corinthians:

> Now there are varieties of gifts, but the same Spirit; and there are
> varieties of service, but the same Lord; and there are varieties of
> working, but it is the same God who inspires them all in every one.
> To each is given the manifestation of the Spirit for the common
> good. To one is given through the Spirit the utterance of wisdom,
> and to another the utterance of knowledge according to the same
> Spirit. . . . All these are inspired by one and the same Spirit, who
> apportions to each one individually as he wills.
>
> For just as the body is one and has many members, and all the
> members of the body, though many, are one body, so it is with
> Christ. . . .
>
> For the body does not consist of one member but of many. If the
> foot should say, "Because I am not a hand, I do not belong to the
> body," that would not make it any less a part of the body. (1 Cor
> 12:4–8, 11–12, 14–15)

So, what can we do? We should follow the gifts that God
has given us (as Saint Paul suggests) and have profound
respect for all the other gifts and members "within the body."
How should that respect be manifest? By encouraging and
supporting ministries of mercy other than our own, and,
through this, to develop the heart of compassion for all who
are served through those ministers and ministries. In this
way a person working with troubled teens might deeply
appreciate a person in prison ministry. Though he may not
have time (or even a talent) to work in prison ministry, he
can encourage and support those who do, and, above all, he
can pray for those who give and receive that ministry. The
Holy Spirit will work through this open heart and deepen its
compassion and love.

The second caveat concerns wisdom in apportioning our
time and commitments. We cannot respond to *every* need

we notice. First, there is the problem of a limited amount of time, physical energy, and psychic energy. Second, there can be conflicts with other commitments that we have prioritized (commitments to family, work, and other obligations). Third, there is the need to reconstitute ourselves spiritually, psychologically, and physically. Saint Ignatius of Loyola discovered various rules for discernment of spirits as well as practical advice for being a contemplative in action (see chapter 5). A summary of how these rules apply to showing mercy may be given in three succinct points.

1.   We should not take on obligations that will significantly detract from or undermine previous commitments to others. Thus, if we have a family, we cannot be serving at the homeless shelter seven days a week so that we are never present to our families (even though service to the poor is intrinsically good). God does not expect us to bilocate or to become "superpersons." He certainly does not want us to undermine our families. Saint Ignatius learned this wisdom firsthand when he found that he could not do well in school while continuing to obligate himself to long hours of prayer and service (which he had done prior to returning to school). Even though he found his prayer consoling, he discerned that God wanted him to study so that he would be able to serve in even greater ways in the future, and this study (which was not *immediately* gratifying) precluded additional hours for prayer and apostolic service.

2.   Works of mercy should not be debilitating. Sometimes we find ourselves growing weary in our response to others' needs. This weariness can be temporary, but sometimes it

leads to discouragement, physical exhaustion, or increases in stress levels that result in physical, psychological, and eventually spiritual debilitation. Such a condition cannot be viewed as the will of God (Who, as Unconditional Love, is seeking precisely the opposite). This is why Saint Ignatius wanted spiritual directors to approve the penances and works of seminarians and even insisted that all Jesuits manifest problems to their superiors if they find that present or future apostolic service is debilitating. Keep in mind that God's intention is to build us up (not to bring us down). He would prefer to be the Messiah (instead of us). If you have difficulty seeing this for yourself, you may want to connect with a good spiritual director who can help you in discernment.

3. The general norm for discernment and choice of apostolic actions might be phrased as follows: If an action leads to an increase in trust, hope, and love, it is probably a good choice. However, if it leads to a decrease in these theological virtues, then it is probably not a good choice.

For example, a woman might see a particular service (say, teaching a religious education class in the parish on weekends) as something that would not undermine her family and other commitments or that would not debilitate her physically, mentally, or spiritually. Yet, she might feel a gradual increase in stress or find herself not spending enough time with her family, etc. After about four months, she begins to get the feeling that God is asking too much, and she begins to lose heart, and, as a consequence, to believe that God really doesn't care about what happens to her ("God only cares about what happens to everybody else"). She then finds herself trusting in God less and even hoping in God less ("Maybe God is totally indifferent to my salvation"). She then begins to experience a decrease in love (she is more impatient, unkind, irritated, unforgiving, angry, etc.—the opposite of the "Hymn to Love" in 1 Corinthians 13).

If this begins to happen to you, *stop. Examine. Discern.* You may have to give up something that you thought was God's will. Remember, God does not want to sacrifice you (in your trust, hope, and love) for any kind of apostolic service. He does not want you to be either a Nietzschean superman or a messiah. Frankly, He would prefer that you not be. The God of unconditional Love could not possibly hold this out as His hope for you. If you cannot believe that, think of it purely pragmatically—who wins if your trust, hope, and love (and, therefore, you in your spiritual being) are completely debilitated—the Holy Spirit or the evil spirit? Enough said. If you find this kind of discernment difficult, you may want to find a spiritual director who can help you with it.

In sum, the Lord desires a heart of forgiveness, compassion, and mercy, a heart that is not indifferent to the needs of others, but can offer a smile, a kind word, and sometimes much more; a heart that tries, within its physical, mental, and spiritual limits, to respond as best it can; a heart that, at the very least, can pray for whatever it cannot heal or rectify; a heart that cares as Jesus does.

V. Blessed Are the Pure of Heart

When Jesus said, "Where your treasure is, there will your heart be also" (Mt 6:21), He showed the intrinsic connection between desire and the heart. Our hearts follow our greatest desires. If we are to understand what Jesus meant by "purity of heart," we will have to delve into the nature of desire, which lies at the center of not only our spiritual lives but also our meaning and identity. Desire has *levels* of purity. It is one thing *intellectually* to select Level 4 to be one's dominant desire. It is another thing to desire Level 4 in one's *heart*; yet another thing for Level 4 to be so natural and habitual that one acts out of it without thinking; and still another thing for one to be so ensconced in Level 4 that one experiences little internal conflict with the other three levels of desire. When this last state occurs, one might be said to have "purity of heart." However, it can also be said that one has partial degrees of purity of heart as one moves toward the final goal. We might translate this very important Beatitude as "blessed are those who desire God and God's will with such purity and clarity that they can effortlessly order all their other desires toward it."

As will be seen in chapter 6, this central Beatitude, this purity of desire (in Level 4) is the objective of contemplative prayer and is the synthesis of contemplation and action. When contemplation in action effects our transformation (*metanoia*), the spontaneous prayer "Thy will be done" has immense power. It can (almost instantly) calm fear, anger, temptation, attachment, and all the other emotions arising out of misplaced or conflictual desire. As we deepen "purity of heart," we will notice that love comes more easily. We do not have to remember things or compel ourselves or fight conflicting desires. We see the needs of love and our spirit responds naturally, as if being drawn to the fulfillment of our heart's greatest and purest desire. Purity of heart lies at the foundation of all the other Beatitudes. It is similar to hungering and thirsting for God's will, for those with purity of heart intensely desire God's will. When it is strong, it leads *naturally* to humble-heartedness, gentle-heartedness, forgiveness, and mercy.

It should also be noted that Level 4 desire, in Jesus' teaching, cannot be divorced from the other Beatitudes. An intense desire to live for God cannot be indifferent to humble-heartedness, gentle-heartedness, forgiveness, mercy, and peace. It certainly cannot lead away from these Beatitudes. Thus, one cannot say, "I am living for God, therefore, I will have to torture you, insult you, and constrain you to accept the Gospel."

In sum, where there is purity of Level 4 desire, there is love, and where there is love, there is humble-heartedness, gentle-heartedness, forgiveness, mercy, and peacemaking. That is why this Beatitude is the objective of contemplation in action, the objective of our lives, and the foundation of the eternal life to come.

VI. Blessed Are the Peacemakers

Jesus' admonition to be peacemakers goes beyond being a reconciler of conflicts, for His term *shalom* is one of the deepest and richest concepts in Jewish culture. In essence, it means perfect communion with God, which implies a perfect state of fulfillment through God. Thus, a "peacemaker" or a "peace-bringer" is one who brings "communion with God," or "fulfillment through communion with God." This fulfillment would include the fulfillment of desires and interior dispositions. In view of this, the first part of the prayer often attributed to Saint Francis seems to express precisely what Jesus means by "a bringer of *shalom*":

Lord, make me an instrument of your *peace*.

Where there is hatred, let me sow love.

Where there is injury, pardon.

Where there is doubt, faith.

Where there is despair, hope.

Where there is darkness, light.

Where there is sadness, joy.

Peacemaking, in this sense, follows directly from the other Beatitudes. Those who desire God with all their hearts and are consequently humble-hearted, gentle-hearted, forgiving, and merciful will naturally convey love where there is hatred, pardon where there is injury, faith where there is doubt, hope where there is despair, light where there is darkness, and joy where there is sadness. If mercy is the disposition of the heart to respond to need, then peacemaking is the response (that is, the fruit of the heart's desire). The merciful heart brings love, pardon, faith, hope, light, and joy.

We may now see a pattern among the six Beatitudes. Though Jesus believed that humble-heartedness is the most important of the Beatitudes, there seems to be a natural progression of the flow of the Beatitudes from one another. Purity of heart (the desire for God) opens upon desire for the *will* of God (hungering and thirsting for holiness). This desire constitutes freedom from more superficial, conflicting desires and allows for the pursuit of humble-heartedness (placing God in the center and making oneself coequal among others). A contemplative life is necessary to sustain and deepen this most important Beatitude. From humble-heartedness flows gentle-heartedness; from gentle-heartedness, forgiveness and mercy; and from forgiveness and mercy, peacemaking in the sense set out by the prayer attributed to Saint Francis. This conversion of the heart lies at the crossroads between con-templation and action. Contemplation awakens, incites, and cajoles this "conversion in the Beatitudes," while "conversion in the Beatitudes" animates the actions of love.

The deepening of conversion (from purity of heart to peacemaking) must occur through the contemplative life, that is, through praise and gratitude to God, opening upon a joy, peace, hope, and trust that sets our hearts free for love. But we are not left to pursue the contemplative life by ourselves; we have the power of the Holy Eucharist and the Holy Spirit to inspire, animate, guide, rescue, and fill us with the presence of the unconditionally loving God. This will be explained in the forthcoming chapters.

VII. God in Light of the Beatitudes

By the end of this book, one hermeneutical principle will be patently apparent, namely, whatever God asks of us He does perfectly, and whatever He does perfectly belongs to His nature. If God asks us to love, then He loves perfectly and is perfect love. If God asks us to forgive, He forgives perfectly and is perfect forgiveness. We can know this because Jesus has elevated love to the highest of the commandments and there is no hypocrisy in Him or God the Father. Furthermore, Jesus reveals the Father to be *Abba* (loving Father) and reveals the love of His Father to be that of the father of the prodigal son (see chapter 7, section VII). To prove this love and to inscribe it in history and in every one of our souls, Jesus gives us the gift of the Eucharist in conjunction with His sacrificial death (see chapter 1). As if this were not enough, He appears to His disciples after His Resurrection and gives *us* His Holy

Spirit. If Jesus Christ is Unconditional Divine Love, and if love has no hypocrisy, if love is the highest commandment, if the Father is *Abba* (the father of the prodigal son), then God the Father, indeed, God the Father, Son, and Holy Spirit, must be perfect, unconditional Love. This means that the triune love of God is the perfect expression of each of the above Beatitudes, and that each of these Beatitudes belongs perfectly to the triune God.

Thus, we might say that Father, Son, and Holy Spirit can empathize perfectly and are perfect empathy (both within their trinitarian relationship and *toward* all of us). They can see the good news *in* us perfectly, and they are the perfect vision of the good news. They give Themselves away perfectly and are perfect gift of self. They can be with us perfectly and are perfect "being with." They are capable of perfect humility and are perfect humble-heartedness. They are capable of perfect gentle-heartedness and are perfect gentle-heartedness. They are perfectly pure of heart and they are perfect purity of heart. They are perfectly forgiving and are perfect forgiveness; perfectly merciful and are perfect mercy; capable of perfect peacemaking and are perfect peace.

Perhaps a simpler way of recognizing this is through Paul's "Hymn to Love" in First Corinthians 13. Inasmuch as God is Unconditional Love, one can substitute the word "God" for the word "love," and then place the unqualified adverb "unconditionally" in front of each attribute of love. We begin with Paul's rendition of the hymn:

> Love is patient and kind;
> love is not jealous or boastful;
> it is not arrogant or rude.
> Love does not insist on its own way;

it is not irritable or resentful;

it does not rejoice at wrong, but rejoices in the right.

Love bears all things, believes all things, hopes all things, endures
all things.

Love never ends. (1 Cor 13:4–8)

This may be transposed in the following manner:

God is unconditionally patient and kind;

God is unconditionally not jealous or boastful;

God is unconditionally not arrogant or rude.

God unconditionally does not insist on His own way;

God is unconditionally not irritable or resentful;

God unconditionally does not rejoice at wrong, but unconditionally
rejoices in the right.

God bears all things, believes all things, endures all things.

God never fails.

If Father, Son, and Holy Spirit really are Unconditional
Love, and They really do possess the above attributes of love
unconditionally, then They warrant unconditional trust and
unconditional hope from us.

If we can have unconditional hope, does that mean that we
are off the hook? Does unconditional hope and trust mean
that God will do *everything* for us? Obviously not. God has
created us with free will and He allows us to use this even in
the very acceptance, rejection, or ignoring of His love! God
will not force us to accept His gift of infinite Love. If we would
prefer to be self-sufficient (and hopelessly empty), God would
respect that free choice. Therefore, it is incumbent upon us,
at the very minimum, to accept God's love, and when we
have fallen away from that love, to ask for His reconciliation

and forgiveness through the prayer of the publican, "God, be merciful to me a sinner!" (Lk 18:13).

The Church respects the unconditional, forgiving Love of God in its doctrine of imperfect contrition, which suggests that the fear of the loss of God is enough to redeem us because the love of *God* is unconditional. Though fear of the loss of heaven leaves much room for future purification of love, it is nevertheless sufficient to move toward salvation—because *God's* love is unconditional. Perfect contrition (done out of love) is of course the ideal because it entails the purification of love manifest in the Trinity's eternal joy.

I had a catechism teacher in the seventh grade who was very adamant about this "minimum" acceptance of God's love (in order to be saved). He noted, "If you're in an airplane and it starts falling out of the sky, you should say your Act of Contrition." We learned the older form of the Act of Contrition, which emphasized imperfect contrition (fearing the loss of heaven and the pains of hell). He emphasized to us that we should be sure to get that line finished (presumably before the plane hit the ground). Then he very gently added, "But then again, you might not want to wait until the plane is falling out of the sky. It might be better to say your Act of Contrition every day; and then again, it might be better not to limit yourself to an Act of Contrition every day, but to say other prayers as well. And then again, it might be better not to limit yourself to those other prayers, but also to try to imitate the heart of Christ." I always thought to myself, "At least I can do number 1 and number 2, so I must be okay." And that became the ground for what I later discovered to be the beauty of unconditional hope resting in the unconditional

Love of God revealed to us by Jesus Christ our Lord. Paul expresses this so perfectly when he prayed for us:

> For this reason I bow my knees before the Father, from whom every family in heaven and on earth is named, that according to the riches of his glory he may grant you to be strengthened with might through his Spirit in the inner man, and that Christ may dwell in your hearts through faith; that you, being rooted and grounded in love, may have power to comprehend with all the saints what is the breadth and length and height and depth, and to know the love of Christ which surpasses knowledge, that you may be filled with all the fulness of God. (Eph 3:14–19)

My seventh-grade catechism teacher spoke truth in a way that someone with my elementary mentality could understand, and I will be eternally grateful to him for it. Yet the ground of that hope was so much more than I could have ever anticipated.

Approaching the Beatitudes (indeed, the entire Sermon on the Mount) seems so utterly daunting. It requires so much transparent authenticity and purity of heart that one might be inclined to believe that one could never get there. If you had to do this by yourself, that would be true. But the fact is, you do not have to do it by yourself. By hoping in the unconditional Love of God, calling upon His unconditional mercy, remaining open to His unconditionally loving grace, and journeying with the Holy Spirit, we all have more than a chance; we all have the assurance that God will do everything and seize every opportunity to bring us (frequently despite ourselves) right into the midst of His heart. How can we best do this? Through the five pillars of the spiritual life—the Holy Eucharist, spontaneous prayer, reflection on the Beatitudes, partnership with the Holy Spirit, and the contemplative life. Yet, if we fall short of the ideal, even far short of the ideal, we must know in our hearts that God in *His* unconditional Love will reach down and bring us up to where we cannot bring ourselves—even through a most imperfect act of contrition. "But thanks be to God, who gives us the victory through our Lord Jesus Christ" (1 Cor 15:57).

Reflection on the Beatitudes cannot be solely a matter of the mind; it must transform the depths of our hearts. This can only occur through prayer. Saint Ignatius Loyola devised a prayer that is ideal for this "reflection of the heart" called the Examen. He considered it to be the center of Jesuit spiritual life along with the Holy Eucharist. It is described in chapter 8, section II.

Chapter Four

Fourth Pillar: Partnership with the Holy Spirit— Peace, Inspiration, and Transformation

Introduction

The Lord has given us a most remarkable gift: the gift of His Spirit, Who is filled with peace, love, protection, unity, inspiration, truth, and life. Jesus told us He would send the Paraclete, Who would remind us of everything He said and would give us a wisdom that would confound our enemies. Saint Paul tells us that the Spirit will enable us to cry out, *Abba*, and will bestow a peace beyond all understanding. As we try to live out our lives as Catholics and Christians, we need to be aware of how our greatest advocate, consoler, protector, inspirer, transformer, and guide works in our lives and how we might be able to work in tandem with His wisdom and love. I will present five general points about the Spirit's workings and how we might coordinate our efforts toward love, the common good, and the kingdom of God:

1. A peace beyond all understanding
2. Inspiration and guidance
3. Transformation in the heart of Christ

4. Working with the Holy Spirit
5. Consolation, desolation, and spiritual discernment (see chapter 5)

I. A Peace Beyond All Understanding

The peace coming from the Holy Spirit is more than mere relief from suffering, a sense of well-being, or a sense of equanimity. It is rooted in a deep sense of home, home amid the cosmos (which we who have faith know is being at home with God). Its opposite is alienation, a sense of not being at home in or "being out of kilter with" the totality. The signature of the Holy Spirit is the sense of having a place in the totality, of "fitting in," of being bathed in joy or light (even when one is aware of sadness and darkness), that is, of being in unity with the Creator and principle of all being.

As Catholics and Christians, we very likely view this "being at home in the totality," this "freedom from being alone in the totality," as "being part of the mystical body of Christ." Being part of Christ's mystical body through the Holy Spirit is an experience of home, holiness, unity, joy, and peace as seen through the eyes of thousands of saints who have embraced a life of holiness throughout history.

I recounted one such experience of the mystical body at Christmas (see chapter 1), and I have had many other such experiences since that time. They have occurred while hearing a bird, hearing truths about the kingdom of God, walking in a thirteenth-century monastery, and celebrating the Holy Eucharist. These experiences are termed "affective consolations" (see chapter 5) and point to the essence of

Paul's "peace beyond all understanding." There are multiple fruits of this peace. I will address only three:

1. Peace in times of suffering
2. Peace in times of persecution
3. The peace necessary for good judgment

1. Peace in Times of Suffering

Have you ever had the experience of being immersed in a tragedy or a troubling or threatening series of events, and, in the midst of these troubles, experiencing a deep sense of calm and assurance that everything is going to be all right? When I was younger I had such experiences of the peace of the Holy Spirit, but I actually tried to talk myself out of them. I remember hearing the news of my father's death, and having this deep and abiding peace and sense that everything was going to be fine. I thought to myself, "I should not be feeling this; this is really tragic; my father was only fifty-nine years old; and furthermore, my mother is probably frantic; and furthermore, my sister is not finished with college; and furthermore . . ." The more the Holy Spirit attempted to intervene with peace, the more I "guilted myself" out of it. I later came to find, through multiple experiences of this "peace in the midst of troubles," that the Spirit was genuinely present, working within my life and the lives of people around me to bring good out of what seemed so negative. My advice is to take the peace and follow the lead of the Spirit, Who assures us that everything is going to be all right. Doing this will give the Holy Spirit room to maneuver through your free will to bring about optimal goodness and love for you, others, the community, and the kingdom of God.

2. Peace in Times of Persecution

Have you ever had the experience of being marginalized,
embarrassed, or even threatened because of your faith or your
loyalty to Christ or the Church? If you're anything like me,
when these situations occur, you might feel a deep dejection,
emptiness, or even a sense of foreboding or evil. These
feelings may debilitate you for a few moments or even cause
disturbance of sleep. As noted earlier, these feelings can be
mitigated by praying the prayer "Thy will be done." The more
I surrender to God through this most efficacious prayer, the
more I sense God's guidance and the more I know that the
persecution perpetrated will result in a better condition for
others, my organization, my community, and, yes, even me.

This sense of confidence about the redeeming love of God
is not a sense that God is going to bail me out of the bad
situation and the bad feelings that accompany it. Rather, it is
a sense of what is promised in the Gospels:

> [W]hen they bring you to trial and deliver you up, do not be anxious
> beforehand about what you are to say; but say whatever is given you
> in that hour, for it is not you who speak, but the Holy Spirit. (Mk
> 13:11; see Mt 10:19 and Lk 21:12)

The Holy Spirit grants us serenity through surrender, and
then guides and inspires. I frequently wake up at three o'clock
in the morning, and the words I need to say are given to me,
and these words (or arguments) are more than sufficient
to introduce truth in the midst of trickery, deception, and
outright falsity. Most of the time these words are convincing,
but even when they fail to persuade opponents, they have a
way of letting light into the world. When one thinks about the
Cross of Christ, one can see that His words did not convince

His opponents, but they did, through the Holy Spirit, let the light of the Father shine before all. As a result, those words let the light of the Holy Spirit, Church, the sacraments, the Sacred Scriptures, the liturgy, and the actions of *agape* flood into the world. In the end, the Holy Spirit will be victorious, even if we, as human instruments, are somewhat baffled as to how and when it will occur.

The interesting aspect of this is the confidence we feel in times of persecution. It is not a confidence derived from our thoughts or planning, for frequently our thoughts leave us bereft of confidence. Neither is it a confidence derived from our natural feelings, for they are filled with foreboding and bewilderment. The source of the confidence? It is the peace beyond all understanding, the grace of the Holy Spirit, Who comforts, protects, guides, and ultimately allows the loving will of God, indeed, the very kingdom of God, to be victorious. It is lovely indeed to have experienced this grace, to have been honored to be an instrument, even if it comes at the cost of persecution. This is why Christ says, "Blessed [happy] are you when men revile you and persecute you" (Mt 5:11).

3. *The Peace Necessary for Good Judgment*

Good judgment is needed because many of our decisions cannot be resolved by mathematical or analytical processes. They require an intuition about the right thing to do, which is developed over the course of hundreds of experiences and relationships. Without peace of mind, this intuition (this essential power of judgment) could be led astray. When it is so led, it could harm people, organizations, and even communities.

If you are anything like me, then you will need the peace of the Holy Spirit to overcome the concerns of egocentricity. Countless have been the number of times when I have gone on an ego trip to the detriment of my good judgment. I recall once being given excellent advice by a subordinate who did not, in my view, adequately acknowledge my "superior intellect." He was simply asserting his opinion as better than my own! This really upset me. Indeed, I found it deeply disturbing and began to think of all the ways in which he had not acknowledged my intrinsic superiority in the past. This led to a reflection about how others had similarly mistreated me. I immediately began to make mountains out of little ego molehills, and the next thing I knew, I could not concern myself with the big decisions of the day or the common good of the organization. I had to allow my psyche to be fully occupied with blame and outrage toward these contemptuous underlings.

The Holy Spirit began to weave His wonderful grace into my heart, but at first I would not listen. It was as though the Holy Spirit were telling me, "Bob, move over and let me drive for a minute," but I had to reply, "I'll get back to You as soon as possible. I need to drive this car into the wall first."

As the car approaches the wall, the Holy Spirit has a way of being more persistent, of calming me down, of gently but firmly guiding me to look at the silliness (or even the potential insanity) of my egoism. He frequently helps me not only to sense imminent tragedy and the embarrassment following from it; He helps me to overcome the embarrassment I feel just before the car hits the wall. For a fleeting moment, I have the peace of good judgment and can apply the brakes with proper apologies.

This experience points to a more subtle, fundamental truth, namely, that the peace of the Holy Spirit helps us to attain good judgment in our decisions, great and small. If we ask for and attend to His peace, which is even embedded in our most egocentric moments, good judgment can return, and that good judgment, under the influence of the Holy Spirit, will lead to the common good, indeed, the optimal good, the good of the kingdom, within the world.

II. Inspiration and Guidance

The Holy Spirit not only provides peace, but also inspiration and guidance. I will consider three aspects of this inspiration, which is by no means an exhaustive list:

1. Words of help and edification
2. The *sensus fidei*
3. Guidance on our way

1. Words of Help and Edification

I might begin with a passage cited earlier: "Do not worry beforehand about what you are to say, but say whatever is given you . . . through the Holy Spirit." The Holy Spirit "gives words" not only in times of persecution, but also for the building of the kingdom and the edification of listeners. Many have been the times when I was inspired to write about a topic, but I could not quite conceive of what to say. I would start writing one simple thesis statement that reflected the direction I wanted to go. Suddenly, words began to come to me. I began to think of additional points that bolstered the thesis statement, additional distinctions that clarified it, stories that animated it, and then good advice that could be drawn from it.

You might immediately conjecture, "Well, that is the normal muse of an author. Why call it 'inspiration of the Holy Spirit'?" I certainly agree that this process does represent an ordinary muse of authorship, but when I read back what I just said and actually derive benefit from it because my writing was more profound than anything I had consciously thought of previously, I must admit I am truly given pause. I find myself asking, "Who said that?" For it really doesn't sound like something I would say. It doesn't sound like my style, and the content seems to have exceeded my limited powers of perception and wisdom. One might say, "Well, your subconscious mind was tacitly aware of all of this, but your conscious mind was not. That is why your conscious mind was genuinely surprised at the depth of content and the beauty of style." Hmm. If my subconscious mind is so smart, how come it doesn't speak more often to my conscious mind so that I might derive benefit from it every day (outside the context of preaching, writing, or helping others)? Why is it that when I am not trying to help someone, I am almost befuddled by my musings, and confused by my subconscious mind? Just curious.

This gives us a clue about how the Holy Spirit of love operates. The usual context is when we're trying to help or edify another person. The Spirit does not blast thoughts into our heads, but rather gives us a thesis statement with a sense of drawing us to something deeper. Now we, in our freedom, must follow this sense of being drawn. If we do, then our desire to help, and our effort to formulate, combine with this sense of following Wisdom, and words begin to tumble out. They may be prosaic or poetic, ordinary or beautiful to behold, plain and straightforward or filled with metaphor and imagination, but whatever the case, they have the capacity to reach into the hearts of deeply empathetic individuals, moving them to new depths and directions of love. Our job is to follow this sense of being drawn, and to exert the effort to put words into what our hearts already seem to know. The Holy Spirit will take care of the rest.

2. *The* Sensus Fidei

The Second Vatican Council's Dogmatic Constitution on the Church, *Lumen Gentium,* declares:

> For by this sense of faith which is aroused and sustained by the Spirit of truth, God's People accepts not the word of men but the very word of God (cf. 1 Th. 2:13). It clings without fail to the faith once delivered to the saints (cf. Jude 3), penetrates it more deeply by accurate insights, and applies it more thoroughly to life. All this it does under the lead of a sacred teaching authority to which it loyally defers. (12, Abbott translation)

What the Council Fathers acknowledge is that when we loyally defer to the teaching authority of the Church, the Holy Spirit grants us deep insight into the truth of faith, which has the capacity to move, transform, and deepen our love and lives. Have you ever had the experience of reading a book or listening to a lecture, and as you were reading or listening, you began to think, "I don't know why this is wrong, but this sounds wrong." You may have gone to the lecture without any suspicion or any knowledge that would have evoked such a thought, yet you feel that there is something wrong, and even disquieting or disturbing. You may have left the lecture preferring not to follow the lecturer's advice and to leave the entire matter aside. Then, five years later you read an article where this precise idea is shown to be contrary to Church teaching or to the love of Christ. You might have thought, "Hey! I knew that five years ago, but I just didn't know why." I believe this sense of disquiet or disturbance is the Holy Spirit protecting us from what could lead to disruption of life and love.

It might be retorted, "Well, maybe all your reading in theology that has congealed in your subconscious mind led you to the discovery of the potential for aberrancy or error. Why call it the Holy Spirit?" I might find this explanation tempting were it not for the fact that I had such experiences prior to doing any significant reading in theology. When I was in high school, I had some fine CCD teachers, but they did not equip me for the ideas I was to confront in college. Yet, I *knew* that there was something wrong with "situation ethics" even though I first found it rather noble and attractive. I wanted to believe that all I needed to do was "seek the greatest amount of neighbor welfare for the greatest number of people," and not have to worry about principles, rules, or anything like that. Yet, I felt a deep disquiet amid the feelings of nobility and simplicity, and I began to sense an error of omission that was not yet clear to my discursive power. It led me to research, then to Paul Ramsey, and then to the revelation that one needs principles and rules to assess the means to even the most noble ends. Without such rules, the end could easily be thought to justify an evil means.

How does one know what one does not know? How does one know *that* one does not know? How does one have the foreknowledge about an error of omission when one does not know all the possibilities? How does one feel deep disquiet while feeling a great sense of nobility? I am not certain of the answer to this, but I have a sneaking suspicion that it is not the efficacy of my subconscious mind. Perhaps the Holy Spirit?

Conversely, have you ever had the experience of reading a book by a spiritual writer (say, article 3 of question 2 of part I of Saint Thomas Aquinas' *Summa Theologica*) and finding yourself absolutely captivated? I have. When I was in college, a friend gave me a used copy of the *Summa* and indicated that I should at least read part of the first part. Though I found the style incomprehensible (with all the counterarguments and the responses to the counterarguments), I felt inspired by these passages. I recall three feelings in particular. First, I felt a genuine sense of being at home with God (similar to the sense of the Mystical Body described earlier). I also had a sense of Saint Thomas' holiness and a desire to be involved in it myself. Thirdly, I felt not so much an awareness that particular propositions were true, but that I was in the presence of Truth itself. At the time, I was not able to articulate these feelings, but I knew that Saint Thomas' writings were not only true but also life-changing. As I read through the unusual style and difficult prose, I felt fed, at home, and desirous of more. Again, given my ignorance at the time, I hesitate to attribute these desires, thoughts, and feelings to some mysterious certitude within my subconscious. Quite frankly, I believe that the Holy Spirit was there inspiring, cajoling, guiding, and filling me with light, delight, and home.

The Holy Spirit will not leave anyone bereft of the disquiet of falsity, or the inspiration of truth. All we need do to experience this deeper, life-changing, efficacious, and loving insight is, as the Vatican Council suggests, to defer to the "teaching authority of the Church," and follow the sense of light, home, holiness, and peace that not only brings joy to the soul, but a wisdom and love quite beyond our natural ability. As usual, the Holy Spirit takes care of the rest.

3. Guidance on Our Way

The Acts of the Apostles are filled with instances of guidance by the Holy Spirit. As one reads the multiple testimonies of Peter, Paul, and the other disciples about how the Spirit guided them to and from specific towns and circumstances, one gets the feeling that the direct experience of the Holy Spirit guiding the Church was almost commonplace (see Acts 8:28–30; 10:18–20; 11:12; 13:4; 16:6–8; 19:20–22; 20:21–23; 21:3–5).

I suppose most people have had the experience of making a "prudential judgment" and then feeling a deep sense of disquiet. As one begins to follow through on the prudential judgment, the disquiet becomes disturbance of soul and even foreboding, and, eventually, one begins to see that the prudential judgment was not prudential at all. The continuous movement from disquiet to discord to disturbance to foreboding can *sometimes* be indicative of the Spirit's guidance. Needless to say, one cannot equate disturbance of soul with the guidance of the Holy Spirit, for there could be many natural reasons for this, for example, insecurity, natural fear, anxiety about associating with certain people, anxiety about the unknown, and so on.

How, then, do we know when disquiet is from the Holy Spirit? By following the best light of our reason and prudential judgment, while keeping attuned to *possible* problems indicated by the sense of spiritual disturbance. If problems arise and become truly precarious, then one might want, not necessarily to reverse one's course of action, but to redirect or redesign it. The objective is to keep both lights (that is, the light of reason and the light of the Holy Spirit's peace) in conformity with one another. If one neglects the light of reason, one could easily be paralyzed by negative emotions. Conversely, if one neglects the light of the Holy Spirit, one can be deceived by rationalization and unforeseen consequences. It is important to note that the Holy Spirit does not in any way want us to ignore the light of reason and prudence, for reason and prudence are also inspired and guided by that same Spirit.

The Holy Spirit can also move one *toward* action through peace, excitement, and zeal. The Holy Spirit can draw one into an opportunity, then open doors into that opportunity, drawing one further into the opportunity through a sense of peace, excitement, and zeal, and then open more doors, and so forth. This favorite "tactic" of the Holy Spirit can happen so quickly that one can find oneself in a whole new dimension of life, marking out whole sections of one's calendar, starting whole new institutes, and writing whole new books before one has had the opportunity to ask how one got oneself into this "fix" in the first place.

I am not suggesting that all manifestations of this tactic are the action of the Holy Spirit, for sometimes one can be *naturally* drawn toward an opportunity, and by *natural* happenstance have doors open, and be drawn into an opportunity further by *natural* feelings of peace, zeal, and excitement. But one can see the "fingerprints" of the Holy Spirit when one finds oneself doing what one was previously disinclined to do, doing it well, and producing considerable spiritual fruit beyond one's highest expectations. Hmm. Could this aggregate of improbable events be more than mere coincidence?

The Holy Spirit also guides us in our long-term plans, vocations, and elections in life. Saint Ignatius tried to show how we might best discern the Spirit's guidance in this regard through his rules for the discernment of spirits in his *Spiritual Exercises*. These will be taken up in chapter 5.

III. Transformation in the Heart of Christ

By now, it is probably clear that the grace of the Holy Spirit is personally transforming. The Spirit's power does not simply *help* us in times of suffering; it *transforms* us as well. The Spirit not only gives us words of faith in times of persecution, but also transforms our capacity for love through that persecution. The Spirit does not merely guide us to opportunities for the kingdom or opportunities to edify, but helps us through zeal, love of the kingdom, and service to grow in faith, wisdom, and love. Thus, the Spirit always has a twofold agenda:

1. The advancement of the human community (in peace, justice, love, the common good, and the kingdom of God)
2. The personal growth and transformation of the individuals advancing the kingdom

How can we cooperate with this twofold agenda of the Spirit? By attending to His "game plan" for bringing personal transformation out of life's successes and sufferings. This is frequently marked by a six-part cycle:

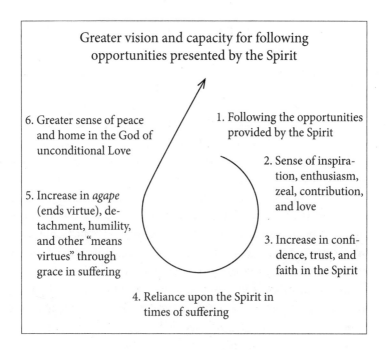

Greater vision and capacity for following opportunities presented by the Spirit

6. Greater sense of peace and home in the God of unconditional Love

1. Following the opportunities provided by the Spirit

2. Sense of inspiration, enthusiasm, zeal, contribution, and love

5. Increase in *agape* (ends virtue), detachment, humility, and other "means virtues" through grace in suffering

3. Increase in confidence, trust, and faith in the Spirit

4. Reliance upon the Spirit in times of suffering

When I follow the opportunities provided by the Spirit and notice some good for the kingdom emerging out of this joint effort (no. 1 in the above chart), I cannot help but feel inspired and filled with zeal (no. 2). It is not merely the sense of contribution, the sense of making a difference to something of ultimate significance, but also a sense of "doing something beautiful for the one I love," as Mother Teresa once said. This inspiration, enthusiasm, zeal, and sense of contribution and love makes the promise of Jesus in the parables (for example, the parables of the talents and the mustard seed) come alive. If we use our faith and act on the opportunities given us to build the kingdom, it will generally lead to an increase in trust (that is, faith—no. 3). The sense of inspiration and enthusiasm, etc., constitutes a history of working well with the Spirit, which leads to an inner confidence that the Spirit really is working with me. This inner confidence, in turn, translates into trust in the providence promised by Jesus Christ.

This trust (built on a history of partnership in building the kingdom) will become a conduit of grace in times of suffering and persecution (no. 4). To the extent that I trust in the Spirit, I will also be able to believe in His providential action working in and through suffering. This trust enables me to bear patiently with suffering when I do not yet see its ultimate meaning or goodness. I genuinely believe that there is meaning and goodness in the suffering, and that if I cooperate with the Lord in prayer, He will effect this goodness in His time and way. When He does this, it will generally produce goodness (for me, the community, and the kingdom) far beyond my highest expectations.

Grace in suffering leads to *personal* transformation. In my experience, the Spirit has brought personal transformation out of suffering in three ways that are directly related to my ability to live the life of the Beatitudes:

1. Leveraging pain to break the spell of bad habits
2. Leveraging pain to give deeper perspective into others' needs, and, therefore, deeper empathy
3. Leveraging pain to produce greater humility (detachment from ego) so that I might live more deeply the life of the Beatitudes

Though suffering is unpleasant, it can produce the fruits of *agape* in ways that no other life experience can. Suffering contains the magic ingredient of "pain leading to new habits." If I cooperate with the Spirit in times of suffering, I can break old habits and form new habits with an incredible freedom. This freedom for "new habits of the heart" leads toward the life of the Beatitudes (no. 5).

For example, with respect to leveraging pain to break bad habits, I can identify several instances in my life where I was being carried along by a momentum that was destructive to both myself and others (for example, self-justified outbursts that no one else thought were justified and intellectual elitism). I had two strikes against me when the bad habits were strong, namely, (1) I believed them to be justifiable, and (2) their momentum was so strong that they prevented me from reflecting on their destructive character.

The wonder of abject pain is its capacity to break down the structure of previously existing beliefs. I am really not a masochist; indeed, I hate pain. Yet, I know that some of the more painful experiences of my life have caused me to doubt thoroughly entrenched destructive belief systems. If I cooperate with the Holy Spirit in this moment of doubt, He can rush in with a new belief system (patterned along the lines of the Beatitudes). The "trick" is for me to be responsive. When I perceive wisdom (particularly the wisdom of the Beatitudes) in ways that I never saw before, I need to be responsive, that is, to embrace the wisdom that will bring me beyond my previous "blindness of convenience and past habit."

However, this is not enough, for I cannot rely on pain (a negative motivator) alone to break the bad habit. Indeed, I really don't want to, because it hurts too much! I then must cooperate with the Spirit to reinforce the good habit through *prayer*. I need to allow the beauty of God's wisdom that is manifest in my contemplative life to move the good habit into a position of dominance in my psyche. Here, the Holy Spirit uses the sense of peace, beauty, awe, love, and home intrinsic to prayer and contemplation to infuse the goodness, beauty, and wisdom of the Beatitudes within my psyche (no. 6).

The above example is really like a dialogue between the Holy Spirit and the suffering person. The Holy Spirit does not cause pain. Pain generally happens through natural causation or human agency. When it does, it is up to the suffering person not to turn inward, but to look for the grace of the Spirit operating through the pain. This grace can normally be found by looking for destructive belief systems that are being called into question by the pain (and by the Holy Spirit). The job of the suffering person is then threefold:

1. Not to become bitter, self-pitying, and closed off, but, rather, to remain open to an adventure of grace
2. To look for the "self-justified," destructive belief system that is being challenged
3. To allow oneself to seriously and deeply doubt that self-justified, destructive belief system

The Holy Spirit will then present the wisdom of the counterposition (the position of the Beatitudes). When the Spirit does this, one will be struck by the rightness and goodness of what was previously thought to be virtually unintelligible. One should not be surprised to hear oneself exclaiming, "I finally understand what is meant by 'the poor in spirit' (that is, the humble-hearted). I'm beginning to see why the poor in spirit are truly blessed. I'm beginning to understand what Jesus was up to and how serious He was about the Beatitudes; they were not intended in a merely metaphorical way; they really are the meaning of life, and are truly *beautiful.*" One might even come to the remarkable conclusion (as I have over multiple occasions) that God really is Unconditional Love, and Jesus really is the Son of God. It was not that I didn't believe this tenet of faith *in my mind* previously, for I had strong intellectual convictions and beliefs. But I really did not understand this truth in my heart of hearts; I did not understand it from the vantage point of love (*agape*). The job of the suffering person at this point in the dialogue is to say, "This is really the meaning of life."

The final stage of the dialogue is to replace negative motivations with positive ones. The main positive motivation for me comes through prayer. When I begin to deepen my belief in and living of the Beatitudes, I see them more deeply in the reading of Scripture and in my loving of the Lord in prayer. When I say, "I love You, and I know You love me," or, "I love the beauty of Your ways and the beauty of Your heart," or, "I want to imitate You in Your love," I understand it, believe it, and intend it in a way that is filled not only with the appreciation of lessons learned through pain, but also with a deep sense of the grace of prayer, which is filled with a serenity, peace, love, and, above all, home that is woven into the experience of contemplation by the Holy Spirit (no. 6 in the above-mentioned cycle). This becomes the foundation for beginning the cycle anew with even greater opportunities for advancing the common good and the kingdom of God, and greater opportunities for embarking on the adventure of personal transformation, contemplation, and *agape.*

IV. Working with the Holy Spirit

By now it might be clear that the Holy Spirit works through a conspiracy of grace. The Spirit gives peace, home, and perspective even in the midst of suffering and persecution; gives inspiration and guidance when our natural insight and logic seem to fail; gives a sense of faith and transcendent knowledge through our deference to Church teaching; and brings deep personal transformation out of suffering and zeal for the kingdom. But the Spirit does not stop there. He works in the hearts of others to cultivate faith, hope, and love; He inspires zeal within our *community*, blows open doors of spiritual opportunity, and creates a *collective* "field of grace," which grows in direct proportion to our cooperation with Him. How can we cooperate with the grace of the Holy Spirit? By remembering two simple thoughts: (1) follow the opportunity manifest in the inspiration of the Spirit, and (2) pray, "Come Holy Spirit, enter the hearts of Your faithful and enkindle in them the fire of Your wisdom and love."

The content of this prayer is self-evident, but the first point merits brief attention. Recall from section II(c) that the Holy Spirit's favorite tactic is to draw us into an opportunity, then open doors into that opportunity, then draw us further into the opportunity through a sense of peace, excitement, and zeal, and then open more doors, etc. When you feel inspired (through peace, excitement, and zeal), when you feel the energy of an opportunity that you might be able to accommodate, when you feel the opportunity to "help build the kingdom of God" and to participate in a little piece of this eternal legacy, follow it. If doors keep blowing open in front of you, and you sense that you can accommodate it without doing damage to your other commitments, then keep following. If people start joining in and a "conspiracy of grace" seems to form around your initiative, and you are not required to undermine previous commitments, keep following it.

However, if you find that following the opportunity is undermining previous commitments, or causing interior disturbance (over the medium to long term), or that doors are not opening, you might reconsider the so-called opportunistic prospect. I have had multiple experiences of following "false leads" in my life. Generally two or more of the above negative signs manifest themselves, and enough doors slam so that I know within about three months that the effort is probably not worth my time, or is meant for somebody else, or is meant to be initiated in the future.

There are many reasons why false leads manifest themselves. Sometimes it is attributable to *me* wanting an initiative to succeed because it's appealing, or it (egotistically) adds to my list of accomplishments, or it is a great idea whose time has not yet come, or it requires a gathering of additional people. Unfortunately, I find that half the time, false leads are attributable to my egotistical motivations. The Holy Spirit tries to warn me, but my ego trip cannot let go. Nevertheless, the Holy Spirit prevails and protects me (even if this should hurt a lot and result in abject failure). I have become better at detecting ego-driven initiatives (through the school of hard knocks, God's grace, and the contemplative life), but it is still a challenge, because opportunity-seeking is always a two-sided coin. Whatever is done for the greater glory of God can also be done for the "greater glory of me" when I try to replace God at the center of my universe or when I just plain and simple want to get another ego-hit from another entry on my list of accomplishments. In any case, you can be sure that the Holy Spirit will try to ward off the bad effects of "ego gone mad," and will try to replace it with gentle peace, a love of the Beatitudes, and a sense of who one really is through the Eucharist, the contemplative life, and, if need be, through the school of failed endeavors.

If, through our spiritual life, we allow the Lord to infuse purity of heart (a desire that He be in the center that motivates a desire for *His* kingdom and will), we may be reasonably certain that the open doors following upon excitement, peace, and zeal will be "our opportunity" (with the Holy Spirit) to be engaged in the noble enterprise of doing our little part to build the eternal kingdom. What could be better than this?

Chapter Five

Fourth Pillar: Partnership with the Holy Spirit (*Continued*)— Consolation, Desolation, and Spiritual Discernment

Introduction

Further precision on "working with the Holy Spirit" may be attained through Saint Ignatius Loyola's rules for the discernment of spirits in his *Spiritual Exercises*. He uses the concepts of "consolation" and "desolation" to reveal the workings of the Holy Spirit or the evil spirit. Before these concepts are explained, it is important to note that discernment is different from prudential judgment. Discernment concerns life decisions (such as a career path, a potential partner in marriage, a vocation, membership in a group, a belief pattern, or a significant change of heart). But prudential judgments concern everyday decisions (such as, "Should we infuse more resources into the project?" or, "Should we close this division?" "Should we have lamb chops for dinner?" "Should we buy a Chevrolet?" and so forth). Prudential judgments generally do not require discernment of spirits (scrutinizing spiritual and affective consolations and desolations to probe the possible actions of the Holy Spirit or the evil spirit) because they only entail "common-sense thinking about one's best interests." Life decisions, on the other hand, do require discernment, for they concern one's journey with God, attitudes toward God, and, consequently, one's disposition toward trust, hope, and love. This will be explained below.

I. Spiritual Consolation and Desolation

Recall the general norm for discernment given in chapter 3, section IV, namely, that decisions, resolutions, and patterns of action that, in the long term, increase trust in God, hope in one's salvation, and love (as described by the "Hymn to Love" in 1 Cor 13) are consistent with the workings of the Holy Spirit and therefore might be termed "spiritual consolations." Conversely, decisions, resolutions, and patterns of action that lead away from trust, hope, and love (in the long term) are inconsistent with the actions of the Holy Spirit and therefore may be termed "spiritual desolations." Saint Ignatius attributes the latter propensities to "the evil one" or "the enemy of our human nature."

For example, if you make a decision about your *life* (such as a particular direction, habit of prayer, career, partner in marriage, vocation, set of ideals, or membership in a particular group), and you notice after a while that your trust in God has diminished, you have increased doubts about your salvation or God's desire to save you, and you are increasing in impatience, unkindness, anger, boasting, rejoicing in "bad news," etc., then you will want to examine the decision you have made with a person (or persons) of spiritual experience and maturity. If you do not feel that you have regressed in your conversion or cannot find any other cause for your spiritual desolation other than the life decision you made weeks ago, you may want to seriously reconsider or tone down that decision. If reversing or "toning down" your past decision causes an increase in trust, hope, and love, then you are probably correct in your adjustment of that past decision.

It is important to note that decisions about "life" can lead to impressions about God, and these impressions, in turn, can lead to even deeper impressions about trust, hope, and love. Thus, a particular decision may cause you, in the long term, to believe one or more of the following: "God is asking too much" or "God is asking *way* too much." "God does not really care." "God just wants us to be pawns in His service." "God is concerned more with other people than with me." "God is sick and tired of me committing the same offenses over and over again." "God hates wimps like me." "God wants me to become a stoic." "God wants me to fear Him more than He wants me to love Him." "God hates a particular group of people." "God is indifferent to my salvation" (for example, God is thinking: "Ah, Spitzer . . . Heaven—Hell—Heaven—Hell . . . Oh . . . Hell. Whatever"). "God is the opposite of the father of the prodigal son, or the opposite of the Good Shepherd (He would rather stay with the ninety-nine righteous ones in the field than go in search of the lost one, who probably deserves to be out there anyway)." "God is the opposite of the characteristics in First Corinthians 13, namely, impatient, unkind, unmerciful, boasting, angry, rejoicing in what is bad, not rejoicing in what is good." "I have finally stepped over the line and God cannot forgive me for this one." "I have to do it all myself, and then, when everything is 'cleaned up,' I can invite God in because He only wants to be in a clean house." "God would rather have me be in despair (because I deserve it) than to live in hope in His unconditional Love." "God wants me to be perfect as fast as possible, even if it does come at the cost of complete debilitation." "God secretly wants me to be scrupulous because it will speed up my progress toward perfection." The permutations of this "logic" are endless.

These *mis*impressions of God, which diminish or restrict His unconditional Love and run contrary to the father of the prodigal son and Jesus' final commandment ("Love one another as I have loved you") can soon undermine trust, hope, and love. They can make us want to avoid God, to run away from God, to hide from God, and to engage in the worst of all possible prayers. "Don't worry, God; I'll get it taken care of any day now, and then, when I do, You can come into my abode." Needless to say, if we need God "to clean up the abode," this prayer will assure that God stays outside, and, therefore, that the abode will never be cleaned up, and, therefore, that God will never be invited inside. This can hardly be thought to be the desire of the *Holy* Spirit.

These unjustified (and incorrect) thoughts and feelings can lead to affective desolation (self-induced dissonance, darkness, and confusion), which, in its turn, can severely undermine the possibility of love. When we feel unloved, it is very difficult to love. When we feel surrounded by darkness, it is difficult to be anything but stoically self-sufficient (which runs counter to love's gift of self). When we feel fear and dissonance, it is difficult to do anything other than turn in on and protect ourselves.

The one thought to remember here is that this cannot be the intention of the Holy Spirit. If the Holy Spirit's goal is to transform our hearts into the heart of Christ (the Beatitudes), then it can hardly be thought that the Holy Spirit would want to create impressions of God or impressions of "my life before God" that would severely undermine trust, hope, and, above all, love. Even if the Holy Spirit were a pure pragmatist (which He is not), it still would make no sense for the Spirit to undermine His supposed purpose—to convert the hearts of mankind to the love of Christ. "A kingdom divided against itself cannot stand." Thus, it is always helpful to test the long-term effects of life decisions through the criteria of trust, hope, and love.

II. Affective Consolation and Desolation

The term "affective" refers to feelings, and so affective consolation and desolation is *felt* consolation and desolation. We will begin with affective consolation.

1. Affective Consolation

Affective *consolation* generally refers to a feeling of God's presence that may be manifest in three ways: (1) elevated consolation, (2) gentle consolation, and (3) ordinary consolation.

1. *Elevated Consolation.* Elevated consolation combines feelings of mystery, awe, joy, home, love, transcendental unity, elation, and sometimes even ecstasy. It is extraordinarily attractive, moves one out of oneself, and imparts a sense of unity with and home in the "totality." It can last for but a second or for long periods of time. C. S. Lewis describes it

beautifully in his well-known work *Surprised by Joy*, named after this profound experience of God:

> The first [experience of God] is itself the memory of a memory. As I stood beside a flowering currant bush on a summer day there suddenly arose in me without warning, and as if from a depth not of years but of centuries, the memory of that earlier morning at the Old House when my brother had brought his toy garden into the nursery. It is difficult to find words strong enough for the sensation which came over me; Milton's "enormous bliss" of Eden (giving the full, ancient meaning to "enormous") comes somewhere near it. It was a sensation, of course, of desire; but desire for what? Not, certainly, for a biscuit tin filled with moss, nor even (though that came into it) for my own past. *Ioulianpotho* [Oh, I desire too much.]—and before I knew what I desired, the desire itself was gone, the whole glimpse withdrawn, the world turned commonplace again, or only stirred by a longing for the longing that had just ceased. It had taken only a moment of time; and in a certain sense everything else that had ever happened to me was insignificant in comparison. . . .
>
> [It is like] an unsatisfied desire which is itself more desirable than any other satisfaction. I call it Joy, which is here a technical term and must be sharply distinguished both from Happiness and from Pleasure. Joy (in my sense) has indeed one characteristic, and one only, in common with them; the fact that anyone who has experienced it will want it again. Apart from that, and considered only in its quality, it might almost equally well be called a particular kind of unhappiness or grief. But then it is a kind we want. I doubt whether anyone who has tasted it would ever, if both were in his power, exchange it for all the pleasures in the world. But then Joy is never in our power and pleasure often is. (Lewis, 1955, pp. 16–18)

One can see in Lewis' description a sense of "home in the totality," or perhaps better, "home in the ageless totality." This home seems to impart a profound sense of peace through the removal of all alienation (from self, others, nature, and even God). It is like a light that outshines all darkness, a warmth that drives out all cold, or a fullness that replaces all emptiness. There is something quite personal and loving in this experience of unity-totality-home, and it is precisely this personal love amid the awe-immensity-enormity that makes it uniquely God's signature. Without the component of awe-totality-unity-immensity-enormity, the personal love would be "nice," perhaps wonderful, but not God. Without the personal love, the awe-totality-unity-immensity-enormity would be terrifying and uncontrollable, but not joy and home. God's signature is in the combination of intimate love with transcendent power, the "joy of home" with immense mystery, delight with the totality of being. As Lewis suggests, the experience brings with it a tremendous "longing for more," a longing to enter more fully into the transcendent mystery that is love-joy-home. When the experience is over, one is left with yet another desire—the desire to experience the desire for God. As such, it is unforgettable.

The experience is truly a surprise. You can be lecturing to a class, hear a bird song outside, and suddenly feel yourself immersed in the unity of all that is—for a fleeting moment, at home with the totality, yet forced to continue the lecture on logic. You might be walking outside and suddenly find yourself walking in the loveliness of Eden, with God presenting each leaf, each rock, each panorama to you with such beauty and awe that literally only poetic expression springs to mind. Even if one is more inclined to math and logic (and is a perfectly awful poet), one cannot help, in the midst of joy, to find the muse of beautiful, metaphorical, incisive expression. You might be reading the Psalms in your breviary, encounter the word "You" (referring to God), and suddenly find your heart filled with such ardor, beauty, and longing that you cannot continue the Psalm but only listen to the echo of the refrain "You." In whatever way you are "surprised by joy," God will enflame desire, and in that desire give an invitation toward home, and in that home offer a unity, joy, peace, and love amidst the totality.

As one grows in the spiritual life and as one's heart progressively becomes purified in the Beatitudes (becoming less and less attached to what is disordered and proud), God transforms the longing into progressively more intense experiences of His *love*. Saint Teresa of Ávila (the sixteenth-century mystic who founded the discalced Carmelites and wrote extensively about the spiritual and mystical life) recounts these experiences of love through the familiar themes of rapture and joy:

> The loving exchange that takes place between the soul and God is so sweet that I beg Him in His goodness to give a taste of this love to anyone who thinks I am lying. On the days this lasted I went about as though stupefied. I desired neither to see nor to speak. . . . [I]t seems the Lord carries the soul away and places it in ecstasy; thus there is no room for pain or suffering, because joy soon enters in. (1976, p. 194)

For Saint John of the Cross (another sixteenth-century Carmelite mystic, also associated with Saint Teresa of the Carmelite order), the unconditional Love of God is manifest most profoundly in the infinite One making Himself our equal in and through His love:

[S]ince He is the virtue of supreme humility, He loves you with supreme humility and esteem and makes you His equal, gladly revealing Himself to you in these ways of knowledge, in this His countenance filled with graces, and telling you in this His union, not without great rejoicing: "I am yours and for you and delighted to be what I am so as to be yours and give myself to you." (1979, p. 613)

This truth (that is, that God would make Himself our equal—as in Jesus Christ—so that we would be better able to love Him in response to His unconditional love for us) seems too good to be true, and so we resist it. Yet, through the presence and consolation of God's love within us, we feel drawn to it as if it is the source of our creation and destiny. And so God wins us over and we begin to know with certainty what He has told us through Jesus Christ His Son, and what He tells us through the Holy Spirit within our hearts: "I am yours and for you and delighted to be what I am so as to be yours and give myself to you."

2. *Gentle Consolation.* Many have experienced the joy described by C. S. Lewis; furthermore, the history of Christian spirituality is replete with examples of joy being linked to the love of God and to our ultimate Home. Yet, profound experiences of this joy-love-home in its enormity and immensity are occasional. It is much more common to experience gentler forms of consolation in our lives of contemplation. Sometimes this experience seems to resemble a *memory* of more intense experiences. Sometimes it seems like a gentle reassurance that God is present and guiding us. Sometimes it is like a subtle hint that the Holy Spirit is nearby. In all cases, though, it is similar to the experiences described above. Though it is only a "hint," it is nevertheless a hint of

the immense, ageless totality amidst personal love, amidst delight and joy, amidst our ultimate Home. Is it possible to have a subtle hint of immense, ageless totality? Yes! I do not know how to describe it other than to say that it happens, and so I pray with Saint Teresa that "I beg Him in His goodness to give a taste of this love to anyone who thinks I am lying." Saint John of the Cross describes this gentle consolation at the conclusion of his work "The Living Flame of Love":

> And thus it is as though the soul were to say: How gentle and loving (that is, extremely loving and gentle) is Your awakening, O Word, Spouse, in the center and depth of my soul, which is its pure and intimate substance, in which secretly and silently, as its only Lord, You dwell alone, not only as in Your house, nor only as in Your bed, but also as in my own heart, intimately and closely united to it. And how delicately You captivate me, and around my affections toward You in the sweet breathing You produce in this awakening, a breathing delightful to me and full of good and glory. (ibid., pp. 643–44)

During my collegiate years, I had several experiences of this gentle affective consolation, but came to recognize what it was only when I went on an Ignatian retreat during my senior year. That retreat ultimately led to my pursuit of a vocation in the Society of Jesus, which entailed a visit to the novitiate. The visit was bizarre, but filled with gentle consolation. When I arrived, the novices were moving from Sheridan, Oregon, to Portland and were in the midst of converting a girls' high school into a novitiate. The only room they had available for a guest like myself was the high school's old paint room. The room was painted a ghastly purple, it stank of paint and turpentine, and it was filthy. A cot was put in the middle of the room and I was told to put my bag in there. When I walked in I was, to say the least, somewhat shocked—but I could not have been happier. I wasn't happy about the room; I was happy being in the novitiate, happy to have found home, filled with a joy quite beyond myself. Nothing—not even that room—could have discouraged me.

I came downstairs, and the novice master invited me out for a walk to talk about my vocation. It was an incredibly icy day. I walked outside and, within a quarter mile of the novitiate, took one of the worst spills of my life. I managed to hit my knee, then hit my elbow, then scrape my hand, but I was incredibly happy, not happy that I had fallen, but happy that I was at home, that God was present, that this was perfectly right. I got back from the walk and met with the novices who seemed to have divergent opinions about everything—but I was happy and at home, and I went to bed in the paint room and experienced a deep elation and peace that simply could not be explained by my surroundings. That's how God can work—gentle, yet filled with His Home and loving signature; persistent but not overwhelming; yet indubitable, indubitably Him, indubitably loving.

This gentle or quieter consolation informs us of the Holy Spirit's presence and guidance. It is a signature of God, and so Saint Ignatius deduced that where it is found, God is also likely to be found. However, this need not always be the case, for one can be deceived by false consolation (see rule number 1 below in section III). For the moment, suffice it to say that God presents us with a gentle sense of totality-joy-home-love (which we may refer to as a sense of deep peace, or absence of alienation, or being at home with the totality) to let us know of His loving presence, to guide us by His Holy Spirit, and to inspire the praise and gratitude that characterizes the contemplative life (see chapters 6–8).

3.   *Ordinary Consolation.* It may not be obvious to you, but our ordinary lives include a dimension of consolation. We frequently do not notice it because we are always experiencing it. I remember a friend in Rome passing by Saint Peter's without even looking up. I said to him, "Hey! You're missing out on Saint Peter's!" He said, "Oh. I see it every day." Sometimes we lose sight of what is beautiful simply because it is commonplace.

However, this ordinary consolation can be easily recognized when it is suddenly toned down or terminated. You may have had the experience of being at someone's house where the radio is constantly on in the background. After a while, you take no notice of it, but when the radio is turned off, the silence is deafening. This also holds true for ordinary consolation. God keeps us bathed in a modicum of peace so that we might be able to carry on our lives with the assurance that darkness will not overcome the light and that hostility will not overcome love. This peace can be disturbed by fear and disappointment arising out of life's ups and downs, but God's peace does not disappear; our faith and contemplative life allow God to bring forth His peace and consolation even amid life's dire circumstances. God gives us this gift out of love, and He intensifies it, strengthens it, and makes it more constant through our faith and contemplative lives.

2. Affective Desolation

Affective desolation is a general sense of *not* being at home in the totality; of being out of kilter with the totality; of being in a cosmic darkness (without warmth); of being alone. These combined feelings can frequently lead to confusion, alienation, and even despondency.

Why would God allow desolation to happen? If we live in ordinary consolation, why would He allow it to cease? Three reasons have typically been given for this by spiritual writers: (1) desolation from lack of conversion, (2) a signal for deeper conversion, and (3) the desert experience.

1. *Desolation from Lack of Conversion.* As noted in chapter 1, section IV, people who are living predominately for Level 1 or Level 2 experience a series of challenges. They feel emptiness or lack of efficacy arising out of living for themselves alone (ego-satisfaction or comparative advantage). They also feel jealousy, fear of failure, ego-sensitivity, blame, contempt, resentment at not being admired by "inferiors," anxiety about not progressing enough (or others progressing more than they), self-pity, and extreme anxiety about being exposed as weak or imperfect. Though Level 1 and Level 2 can bring considerable gratification and excitement, the above negative emotions frequently follow in their wake and can intensify with the passage of time.

These negative emotions could be viewed as desolation— indeed, they are; but they do not have a divine origin, for they are self-induced through choices or failure to make a choice beyond Level 1 or Level 2 default drives. For Saint Ignatius, these desolations will persist until the individual moves to what I term Level 3 and ultimately to Level 4. When conversion (or even deepened conversion) takes place, many individuals experience almost immediate relief from an oppressively negative psychic condition and gain a terrific creative spiritual energy frequently referred to as "first fervor." Thus, one might say that the solution to Level 1 or Level 2 desolation is initial conversion to God (belief in or trust in God sufficient to begin the journey of faith).

2.   *A Signal for Deeper Conversion.* As by now may be evident, those who have made an initial conversion will probably not have attained the fullness of the Beatitudes. Initial conversion puts us on the road, but it does not get us to the goal. Thus, our conversion (*metanoia*) must be deepened throughout our spiritual journey. Sometimes the impetus for this deepened conversion takes place out of natural suffering in our lives. For example, something goes terribly wrong, and I find myself having to deepen my faith and live the Beatitudes more profoundly in order to emerge from this bad situation.

Sometimes desolation can emerge from a *natural* feeling of emptiness. It could arise out of failure to fulfill my higher desires and purpose. I might be living Level 3 very superficially or living Level 4 without any attendance to the Beatitudes or the contemplative life. The emptiness I feel is a natural call to move higher or more deeply into Level 3 or Level 4.

Sometimes, however, the move to deeper conversion does not arise out of *natural* suffering or emptiness. It is induced by a feeling of loneliness, darkness, or alienation within the cosmos or totality, from ordinary consolation being "turned off." This cessation of ordinary consolation is generally the Holy Spirit's signal for us to examine our lives and to embark on deeper conversion. This might entail greater detachment or freedom from Level 1 or Level 2 gratifications, for we can slip into Level 2 interpretations of Level 3 and Level 4 (for example, "I'm doing more good than you are" [Level

3], or "I'm holier than you are and am doing far more for the kingdom than you are and am far more valuable to God than you are" [Level 4]. Yikes!). This desolate signal may also be a call to a greater appreciation or awareness of the Beatitudes, or even a call to a deepening of one's spiritual life. It is important to remember that the Spirit's "turning off of ordinary consolation" is generally not a chastisement, but rather a "wake-up call" (or perhaps even a gong) to alert us to the potential for regression or death, or for greater progress, life, or grace. When it occurs, we should be attentive to it, seek out the possible reasons for it, and try to respond with a gradual realistic plan to deepen our conversion (with the grace of God).

3.   *The Desert Experience.* Since the time of the Old Testament prophets, the experience of "being led out into the desert" has been well noted. The common expression "dryness" or "aridity" in prayer frequently refers to a lack of elevated or gentle consolation (but not necessarily a lack of ordinary affective consolation). The desert experience is generally not linked to a "lack of conversion" or a "signal to deeper conversion." Rather, it is God's way of inducing trust in and surrender to Him without the inducement of *affective* consolation.

Why would God want to deepen our trust and surrender in this way? If He intends to bestow eternal joy (eternal elevated consolation) upon us all, why wouldn't He just use consolation to induce trust and surrender? Because He wants that trust and surrender to arise out of *our* desire for His heart, His way, His love, and His person, rather than out of a desire for consolation, rapture, or ecstasy. At some point in the spiritual life, God has to wean us off of consolation long enough so that our surrender to Him can be *authentically ours*. The difficulty with consolation is that it is so extrinsically attractive that we would do anything to get it. This has the peculiar effect of leaving *our choice* to surrender in question or even in abeyance. Since God would not have us leave this most authentic part of ourselves behind, since He would not let us keep this most important decision of our lives and our essence in abeyance, He either has to turn off or has to tone down His affective consolation so that we might be able to choose (in authentic freedom) to follow Him for His own sake and for the sake of His life and love. Speaking for myself, I could become so "hooked" on consolation that I would not be able to think of anything like authentic love, humility, gentle-heartedness, the "right thing to do," the imitation of Christ, and certainly not the Cross, in my pure surge to move closer to the profound joy of God. I could easily forget God while concentrating on the joy intrinsic to Him.

So God, in His mercy (and His profound respect for us and for our freedom), leads us out into the desert. Sometimes that desert has times of ordinary consolation, sometimes it does not. Sometimes it is a month of aridity, and sometimes (as is occasionally the case with contemplative sisters or monks) it is a long-lasting "dark night of the soul" or "dark night of the spirit." In all cases, God is in charge and knows what we need. Our job is to follow Him out into the desert, to trust Him, to surrender ourselves faithfully to His heart and to wait for the coming of consolation. Indeed, consolation will come, for God will not allow us to stay in the desert one second longer than is absolutely necessary for our freedom, authenticity, and love. Trust Him.

III. Three Rules for the Discernment of Spirits

Saint Ignatius of Loyola recognized that affective consolation and spiritual consolation frequently run hand in hand, but not always; so also with affective desolation and spiritual desolation. Hence, he saw the need to formulate rules for the discernment of spirits. The rules might be summarized as follows:

Rule number 1: *Be attentive to false consolations.* Affective consolation is usually the work of the Holy Spirit, unless it leads to a decrease in trust in God, hope in salvation, or love (in the long term). Thus, you should follow *affective* consolation (a feeling of transcendent peace-home-unity-love-joy) unless it causes long-term *spiritual* desolation (a decrease in trust, hope, and love). If spiritual desolation persists, you should stop following the seeming consolation, for it is very likely a false consolation induced by "the enemy of our human nature." You would then be well advised to make an examination of the decisions, attitudes, or actions that led to the false consolation. It is usually a good idea to do this with a person (or persons) of spiritual experience and maturity. If there does not seem to be any reason for the false consolation other than a particular past decision or course of action, you will probably want to make changes in that decision (see section I).

Rule number 2: *Never make a "life decision" in time of affective or spiritual desolation.* Both affective and spiritual desolation can impair judgment and induce confusion and sadness. As such, desolation will almost always impair or adversely affect long-term life decisions, which are difficult to grasp even in the light of spiritual consolation. For this reason, Saint Ignatius counseled that you should never make a life decision in times of desolation (either affective or spiritual desolation). He hastened to add that desolation will soon give rise to consolation, at which point one can resume the process of making life decisions. It is always worth the wait.

The shortness of this rule should not be construed to indicate a lack of importance. It is absolutely fundamental for good spiritual judgment and progress in the spiritual life. Some followers of Saint Ignatius considered it *most* essential.

Rule number 3: *The evil one can come as an "angel of light."* As Saint Ignatius implies, the devil usually dissuades us from our good intentions by trying to discourage us. Sometimes this can be accomplished by temptation (particularly temptations toward the seven capital sins), spiritual desolation (undermining trust, hope, or love), nightmares, or by playing to other fears; but sometimes he appears in his role as deceiver. In this case, he comes offering a thought that *appears* to build up the spiritual life. It seems to be consistent not only with affective consolation but with spiritual consolation. It plays to our desire for deeper conversion, and it can be overtly pious or "holy." However, the real intention is to *discourage* us in the intermediate to long term. This discouragement can frequently dash expectations, cause frustration, and lead to a decrease in trust, hope, and love (spiritual desolation). Some illustrations may help.

Suppose you are in spiritual consolation. Your trust in God has increased, and along with this your hope in salvation and your appreciation of the Beatitudes. You are in a state of fervor toward improving your spiritual life and your love of neighbor.

In the midst of this fervor, you think to yourself, "If a half an hour of daily prayer is good, then three hours must be better." You begin your new discipline and find yourself growing progressively tired. You do not have enough time for your family and work, and even though the fruits of your prayer are good, you find yourself snapping at people or even thinking that *they* should be spending three hours in prayer (because you are making such a great sacrifice to do so). After a while you start believing that God really *expects* this of you, yet you feel like you cannot continue without dissolving emotionally and ruining your family. You begin to think, "God is asking too much of me and He is not giving me the graces I need to continue this good and holy discipline." You begin to have a view of God as a stoic taskmaster, of your family as unappreciative spiritual "do-nothings," and your workplace supervisors as completely unfair. You keep thinking to yourself, "But I'm doing this for God!" When the collapse takes place (and it generally does), you find yourself frustrated, discouraged, cynical, and on the brink of despair. What happened? The evil one came disguised as an angel of light and pushed you beyond your limits, beyond what was prudent, and, needless to say, beyond the guidance of the Holy Spirit.

There are many other commonplace scenarios. For example, when I am experiencing spiritual consolation, the thought may occur that I can get rid of the sin of pride tomorrow. "Indeed, I think I can get rid of all sinful inclinations tomorrow!" When I am in a state of consolation, it is quite easy to ward off temptation. However, as the consolation diminishes, I find myself slipping back into the old modes of conduct—blaming others, pandering for praise or respect, seeking status as an end in itself, etc. I am absolutely bewildered. "I thought I had it licked." Discouragement soon ensues, and along with it (as the evil one hopes) cynicism and perhaps even despair.

You will probably notice that the tactic of the evil one is to take something perfectly good and then *exaggerate* it to the point where it is either "over the top" or unaccomplishable. How do these exaggerations occur? In four major ways:

1. Inspiring you to do too many tasks of conversion or perfection ("I think I can tackle greed, lust, *and* pride within the next couple of months")
2. Inspiring you to decrease your timeline ("I think I can attain purity of heart *tomorrow*")
3. Inspiring you toward perfection on your own, as in the worst possible prayer: "Don't worry, God; I'll get perfection taken care of any day now, and then You can come into my soul and be pleased with what I have accomplished"
4. Inspiring you to impute stoic intentions onto God when reading Scripture, doctrine, or tradition ("Spitzer, this is God speaking. Why haven't you become perfect as your heavenly Father is perfect? It is set right out for you in Scripture; and, by the way, why aren't you loving other people as I have loved you? You're slipping up so much that I'm getting tired of waiting. And, frankly, why were you distracted today in your meditation after Communion? . . . And . . .")

Another related (but seemingly opposite) tactic of the "angel of light" is discouragement arising out of increased awareness of ulterior motives. Seminaries are filled with good individuals who began their spiritual journey with a genuine desire to serve God and others. They were moved by zeal for God's kingdom; they had a genuine love of Scripture, doctrine, and tradition; and their intentions were reinforced by affective and spiritual consolation. Then, some years after entering the seminary, they discover, in a remarkably lucid moment, that they had a variety of ulterior motives for entering ("I really didn't want to be a public accountant anyway. The breakup with my girlfriend was overwhelming; and, after all, entering the seminary really did please my mother," etc.). These motives could very well *have been* present, but might be irrelevant to the seminarian at the time when he is thinking about them. Nevertheless, the "angel of light" sees a fantastic opportunity that can lead, with a little push, to discouragement and perhaps even despondency. "You hypocrite. The *only* reason you entered was to escape from what you did not want to do, and to win favor with your family and friends. Your whole vocation is a sham. If you had any integrity or authenticity, you would drop this pretense and go back to public accounting."

Saint Ignatius gives sage advice to us in these situations. First, be very hesitant about giving up something that you *believe* you started for an authentic reason (in the consolation of God) when the *only* things you can see clearly are your ulterior motives. When your vision is restricted to ulterior motives or to negative data (and you *believe* that this was not the case at the time you set out on your journey), then you are likely experiencing spiritual desolation. When you cannot remember consolation, it generally indicates that you are in desolation. Exaggerated negativity about yourself and your intentions (when you are on the road to conversion) is generally untrue and therefore is a marker of spiritual desolation. You must go back to the second rule (given above) when this occurs: "Never make a life decision in times of desolation." The key word here is "wait." Until when? Until you can clearly remember and appreciate the thoughts and consolation that you *believe* you experienced at the time you made your decision.

When we discover that good, holy, or pious intentions are (in the intermediate to long term) turning into spiritual desolation (decrease in trust, hope, and love), then we will want to reexamine those thoughts, decisions, or resolutions as quickly as possible. As noted above, it is helpful to do this with a person of spiritual experience or maturity. It helps to have people point out what we already suspect (in our most rational moments) to be highly inadvisable. Why? Because we can be stubborn. ("I thought this was a good idea last week, and so it still should be a good idea today—even though it's killing me"). Or we might think that everything we start with a pious intention must be God's will ("I believe the Holy Spirit inspired me to attain perfection by the end of the week; it must be God's will"). Or we told our friends about desires to deepen our conversion and spiritual lives (and they might think that we're hypocrites if we do not follow through—even though it's affecting us badly).

If we find that our pious decision or resolution might be an exaggeration (a deception of the "angel of light"), then we ought to modify it. Frequently it is not necessary to give up the pious intention, but only to "ratchet it down several notches" in order to make it correspond to our potential and to the Holy Spirit's will and timetable.

These three rules certainly do not exhaust Saint Ignatius' writings (or the contemporary literature) on discernment of spirits. I give these three particular rules because they have come up most frequently in my life and the lives of others with whom I am associated. Hopefully they will be useful for your own spiritual life.

Chapter Six

Fifth Pillar: The Contemplative Life, Getting Started—Building a Contemplative Base

Introduction

The contemplative life is meant to catalyze the heart of the triune God within us. This "Heart speaking to heart" purifies Level 4 desire (purity of heart), which, in its turn, frees us for the other Beatitudes. The Holy Eucharist and the Holy Spirit quicken this grace of the contemplative life. The contemplative life is a conduit between God's inspiring grace (through the Holy Eucharist and the Holy Spirit) and our transformation in the Beatitudes and our graced participation in action.

So what is this contemplative life? Though part of the answer is given earlier in the chapter on the Beatitudes (chapter 3), further elucidation should be provided in three areas:

1. Building a contemplative base (this chapter)
2. Ignatian contemplation (chapter 7)
3. Contemplation in everyday life (chapter 8)

Our awareness and appreciation of God's love frees us to love God and one another. When we see the deep goodness and beauty of God's love and sense His loving presence more deeply, we become free to follow His way (the Beatitudes) and His will (His loving heart) in our lives. This gives rise to a sense of "being at home with God," which is at once a relief from alienation (particularly self-alienation), a sense of peace and unity with the totality (God and everything governed by God), and an openness to guidance by the Holy Spirit toward the fullness of love.

Contemplation is essentially an *opening* of one's self to a deeper and bigger reality. Religious contemplation is opening oneself to the infinite reality of God. It is different from spontaneous prayers that are asking for something specific within the activities of everyday life, for contemplation does not seek, per se, relief, help, forgiveness, inspiration, guidance, "good in suffering," or the fulfillment of a specific need, but rather "simply" to know God more deeply. It is not oriented toward "getting something in this world or for this world." It seeks to know the heart of God, that is, to appreciate God in and for Himself. Since we cannot wrap our minds around God, we must be led by God Himself more deeply into His heart. This occurs through spiritual insights, consolations and desolations, a feeling and awareness of God's love, and an understanding of how to live that love in the world.

This process of being led into the heart of God (by God) generally requires both time and silence and so is best initiated and deepened by a *retreat*. Though one can obtain remarkable contemplative insight from prayer and theological study, an investment of at least three or four days in a contemplative retreat (such as a shortened form of the Spiritual Exercises of Saint Ignatius) can provide a vehicle to let God lead us more deeply into His heart. Contemplative depth requires getting some separation from the colossal busyness of life. Though our busy, goal-oriented, efficiency-driven, computer-cellular-internet culture enables us to accomplish so many things (for our families, churches, organizations, communities, and culture), it keeps our minds and hearts *on the surface.* We are making so many decisions, reacting to so many stimuli, and absorbing so much data, that we cannot allow ourselves a few moments to go into the depths of our hearts, to appreciate the love of God, and to act out of that love in our lives. It is not that we find the contemplative awareness of God threatening or boring or unworthy of our time—quite the contrary; we know deep down that we would find it quite interesting, indeed, fascinating and very much worth our time and energy. But we just can't seem to find the time, and because "the time just doesn't seem to exist," we haven't given ourselves sufficient space to see how lovely contemplating on God's love and mystery can be, how interesting and beautiful giving praise to God can be. And so we "kind of give up"; we make do with half a life, half a heart, and half the loveliness of life in God's love.

This is where a *contemplative retreat* can help, as distinct from a more social, work-driven, or conference-oriented retreat. First, a retreat provides distance from one's hub of activities. Retreat directors try to guide participants toward the mystery of God and help them to let go, for a moment, of the concerns to which they must return. Retreat houses generally provide a place of beauty and serenity so that one might give time to one's deepest thoughts, and through this, free oneself to reflect on the mystery of divine love.

If one cannot break free for even a weekend retreat, then one may want to try "The Spiritual Exercises in Everyday Life" (a special form of the Spiritual Exercises for people who cannot make a retreat), or some other contemplative practice that has sufficient structure and direction to deepen awareness of the love of God. However, I believe that retreats are much more incisive opportunities than these alternatives for God to work wonders within our hearts and lives. Over half the people I have directed on retreats have made time to do additional retreats every year or every other year after the first, because they have developed a longing for the separation from busyness, for depth of reflection, and for time to enjoy the beauty and mystery of God. If you make a first retreat, prepare yourself, because you are likely to make many more. God has a way of drawing us more deeply into Himself even when we think we don't have time.

In chapter 8, I speak about contemplation in everyday life arising out of the praise and appreciation of God in the Psalms, biblical readings, and prayer. I cannot emphasize enough how building a contemplative base (through a deepened awareness of the love of God in retreats or other contemplative spaces) can deepen and magnify the peace, home, love, and light hidden within the words of these psalms and prayers. An investment in one or two retreats can considerably deepen one's everyday contemplative prayer.

Not all retreats are *contemplative* (oriented toward deepening the contemplative life). However, the Spiritual Exercises of Saint Ignatius (which may be found in books available at most Jesuit retreat houses and in many Jesuit universities throughout the world) are specifically geared toward contemplation. There are also other non-Ignatian contemplative retreats. If you are looking for a retreat to build a contemplative base, you will want to make an explicit inquiry of the retreat facility or the retreat director.

As I noted above, the contemplative life is grounded in a deepening awareness of the love of God. Saint Ignatius recommended four areas in which this love is most acutely manifest (and therefore provides content for contemplation on retreats and in other contemplative prayer times: (1) creation around us, (2) creation of our human souls, (3) redemption in Jesus Christ, and (4) the presence and guidance of the Holy Spirit in our lives. Each of these areas merits attention.

I. Creation

You might begin with looking at the beauty, serenity, and "at-home-ness" of nature. Each aspect of nature presents itself as a gift of God within a contemplative setting. Thus, the beauty of a bird's song, a flower, or even a leaf; the glory of a sunrise over the mountains or ocean; the wonder of God's creatures in their natural habitats, all reveal the love and care God has in creating them and even presenting them to us for our delight. The greater our contemplative depth, the more God can reveal His mind, delight, care, and love through creation. A squirrel can be a very interesting revelation of God's delight, the Milky Way a revelation of His mind and grandeur, the friendliness of nature (instead of hostility) a manifestation of His care. When we recognize God's hand presenting all these things to us, making a home, as it were, for us, we can begin to see the simplicity and complexity of His love.

You may go as deeply as your learning allows. You may want to think about the Penrose number—that the odds against our universe being able to sustain any life form are $10^{10^{123}}$ to 1, which is so incredibly improbable that it makes the occurrence of our universe a veritable miracle! (see Penrose, 1989, p. 344). You may want to think of the perfection in which seventeen of our universal constants have been designed so that if their quantities had been altered by even a miniscule amount, the universe could not have evolved into a state allowing the development of a life form. You may want to consider the observations of some of the most notable physicists of the twentieth and twenty-first centuries. The famous astronomer Fred Hoyle concluded through his investigation of the carbon atom, after years of agnosticism, that the existence of God was probative, if not inevitable:

> Would you not say to yourself, "Some super-calculating intellect must have designed the properties of the carbon atom, otherwise the chance of my finding such an atom through the blind forces of nature would be utterly miniscule?" Of course you would. . . . A common sense interpretation of the facts suggests that a superin-tellect has monkeyed with physics, as well as with chemistry and biology, and that there are no blind forces worth speaking about in nature. The numbers one calculates from the facts seem to me so overwhelming as to put this conclusion almost beyond question. (Hoyle, 1981, p. 8)

Arno Penzias, who was co-discoverer of the 2.7°K univer-sally distributed radiation (a remnant of radiation from the originative universe), also declared:

> Astronomy leads us to a unique event, a universe which was created out of nothing, and delicately balanced to provide exactly the conditions required to support life. In the absence of an absurdly improbable accident, the observations of modern science seem to suggest an underlying, one might say, supernatural plan. (Brock, 1992, cited in Bradley, 1998, p. 40)

Robert Jastrow, former head of NASA's Goddard Institute of Space Studies, also noted:

> The scientist has scaled the mountains of ignorance; he is about to conquer the highest peak; as he pulls himself over the final rock, he is greeted by a band of theologians who have been sitting there for centuries. (Jastrow 1978)

Many other famous physicists and astronomers have made such declarations. You may want to refer to my manuscript *New Proofs for the Existence of God: Contributions of Contemporary Physics and Philosophy* (chapters 6 and 7).

From the simplest contemplation on the delight and beauty of nature to the most complex consideration of the equations of astrophysics, God's hand—God's loving hand—reaches forth and presents us with not only home and beauty, but majesty and glory; not only the wonder of this universe, but the more incredible wonder of His life and kingdom to come.

II. Creation of Our Human Souls

More wonderful than the creation of the universe is God's creation of the human soul in the very image of Himself. Not only prophets and holy men recognized this, but also philosophers and scientists. Since the time of Plato, philosophers have recognized five special desires within human consciousness: the desire for perfect and unconditional Truth, Love, Goodness, Beauty, and Being. Plato was so amazed by the human capacity to appreciate the perfect and unconditional that he used it to prove the immortality of the soul. Saint Augustine believed that these desires could not be explained by anything except the presence of God (the perfect and unconditional One) to us. In view of this, he declared, "For Thou hast made us for Thyself, and our hearts are restless until they rest in Thee."

The annals of contemporary philosophy and science are filled with the inexplicable boundary-lessness of the human desire for truth, love, goodness, beauty, and being, and it is by these very powers that we are drawn, if not compelled, to seek out their source. But we need not stop at the *intellectual judgment* that we have a transcendental nature, or that this transcendental nature cannot be fully explained by physical or algorithmically finite structures. We can proceed, through these very powers, to a deep appreciation of their source (Truth, Love, Goodness, Beauty, and Being Itself), and then proceed to marveling at the love of that Source Who created us in His image to be fulfilled, and be filled with joy, by His very presence. We may marvel too at the destiny for which that loving God created us (with a nature that could only be satisfied by Him, a destiny that made Plato conclude to immortality and made Saint Augustine conclude to eternal Love). When we consider the *unconditional* Love, the *eternal* destiny, the *transcendental* soul in which and for which we were created, we will want to say with the psalmist:

> O Lord, our Lord,
> how majestic is your name in all the earth!
> You whose glory above the heavens is chanted
>   by the mouth of babies and infants,
> you have founded a bulwark . . .
> When I look at your heavens, the work of your fingers,
>   the moon and the stars which you have established;
> what is man that you are mindful of him,
>   and the son of man that you care for him?

Yet you have made him little less than the angels,

and you have crowned him with glory and honor.

You have given him dominion over the works of your hands;

you have put all things under his feet,

all sheep and oxen,

and also the beasts of the field,

the birds of the air, and the fish of the sea,

whatever passes along the paths of the sea.

O Lord, our Lord,

how majestic is your name in all the earth! (Ps 8)

And still more, we are *unique* (like our fingerprints) in our transcendentality. God has made us not only with a soul, but He has made that soul unique in its expression of transcendentality. We are "little" unique expressions of the desire and capacity for unconditional Truth, Love, Goodness, Beauty, and Being. When our unique expressions are placed together (through God's unconditional Love and our loving actions), we create a literal symphony of complementary, melodic, harmonious notes (unique expressions) of love and the other transcendentals. This symphony (in its perfect empathy) induces a joy that seems to make time stand still. It may be analogized by an experience most of us have had, namely, going to someone's home or a restaurant and becoming so engrossed with one's friends (not merely in the conversation but in *being with* the friends themselves) that time seems to slip away. Finally, one of the people at the table observes, "It's two o'clock in the morning! Where did the time go?" Indeed, where does time go in the midst of friendship and love? When we realize the uniqueness of our transcendental souls, the complementary role we play in relationships with one another, and the symphony of love for which we are destined, we may again delight in, marvel at, thank, and give praise to the Source, Who created it all. Once again, we are presented with the objective of contemplation. The more we recognize our unique and irreplaceable part within the symphony, the more we delight in the loving God Who predestined it.

III. Redemption in Jesus Christ

Though the creation around us and the creation of our unique transcendental souls is wonderful to behold, it still does not reflect the fullness of God's plan for us. God knew that even with our transcendental souls, we would not be able to reach Him (Who is the fulfillment of our souls) by ourselves. As so many saints discovered in their lives, we cannot leap the infinite gap between our "potential to be filled by perfect Love, Truth, Goodness, Beauty, and Being" and God (the actuality of Truth, Love, Goodness, Beauty, and Being Itself). Some of us may have even attempted to bring ourselves to perfection so that God would be pleased with "our accomplishment." We might have felt the incipient, if not full-blown despair arising out of this undoable project. Emptiness, a sense of incapacity, a recognition of the inauthenticity and pretension of our so-called accomplishment, hundreds of little (and sometimes great) failings, and a sense of an ever-widening abyss between ourselves and our destiny may have finally induced us to say, "Help!" Perhaps someone came into our lives and indicated that our project was not only futile but dangerous and perhaps showed us that what we really need, indeed, *who* we really need, is Emmanuel, "God with us." If God does not come to us and reveal His unconditional Love for us, we would really never believe it. We would probably hold ourselves hostage to Murphy's Law, intoning, "It is simply too good to be true—I cannot bring myself to my transcendental end, and God would probably not care enough about me to help me. And so my life and even my very soul seems to be absurd."

Yet, there is good news. There is a revelation in Emmanuel, a revelation of a God Who not only came to be with us, but to reveal that He is Unconditional Love, and that He would give Himself totally to us and send His Spirit to bring us to Himself. The good news may at first seem too good to be true. Yet, that very Spirit of Love operating in the world calls us to the truth of that Love, the truth of Emmanuel, the truth of Jesus Christ. The deepened affirmation and understanding of the beauty of the truth and beauty of this revelation is precisely the object of contemplation, for it not only brings the truth of the creation of our souls into intelligible fruition (away from absurdity), but also reveals the truth of our eternal destiny in the One Who has loved us so. The following six questions may help to elucidate this.

1. *What is the most positive and creative power or capacity within me?* At first glance, you might want to respond that this power is intellect or artistic creativity, but further reflection may show that the capacity to apprehend truth or knowledge, or to create beauty, *in and of itself*, is not necessarily positive. Knowledge and beauty can be misused; therefore they can be negative, destructive, manipulative, inauthentic, thus undermining both the individual and common good. There is but one human power that contains its own end of "positivity" within itself, one power that is directed toward the positive itself, and therefore one power that directs intellect and artistic creativity to their proper, positive end.

As may by now be evident, that power is love. Love's capacity for empathy and its ability to enter into a unity with others, leading to a natural "giving of self," forms the fabric of the common good and the human community, and so seeks as its end the good of both individuals and that community.

Now, if you affirm the existence of this power within yourself and you further affirm that it is the guiding light of both intellect and creativity, and that its successful operation is the only true way to attain happiness and fulfillment, then you will want to proceed to the second question.

2.   *If love is the one power that seeks the positive in itself, and we are made to find our purpose in life through love, could God (perfect Being), Who created us with this loving nature, be devoid of love?* Love, by its very nature, unifies, seeks the positive, orders things to their proper end, finds a harmony amidst diversity, and gives of itself (creates) in order to initiate and actualize this unifying purpose. This means that perfect love is perfect positivity, which would seem to be consistent with perfect, unconditioned, and creative Being.

This insight into the Creator (that is, that the Creator is Love because a creative act is pure positivity, and love by its very nature is also purely positive) seems to be confirmed by the fact that the Creator has created us not only with the desire for unconditional Love, but also with the desire for unconditional Truth, Goodness, Beauty, and Being.

If the Creator is devoid of love, why would that Creator create human beings not only with the capacity for love but to be fulfilled only when they are loving? If the Creator is devoid of love, why make love the actualization of all human powers and desires, and therefore of human nature? If the

Creator is not loving, then the creation of "beings meant for love" seems absurd. However, if the Creator *is* Love, then creating a loving creature (that is, sharing His loving nature) would seem to be both intrinsically and extrinsically consistent with what (or, perhaps better, "who") He is. Could the Creator be any less loving than the "loving nature" He has created?

If you can reasonably affirm the love of the Creator from the above, then you may want to proceed to the third question.

3. *Is my desire to love and to be loved merely conditioned, or unconditional?* We not only have the power to love, but also a "sense" of what perfect Love would be like. This sense of perfect Love has the positive effect of inciting us to pursue ever more perfect forms of love. However, it has the drawback of inciting us to *expect* ever more perfect love from other people. If you find yourself unable to be ultimately satisfied by any form of conditioned or finite love, then you will have also affirmed your intrinsic desire for unconditional Love as the ultimate satisfaction of your being. This affirmation leads to the next question.

4. *If my desire for love can only be ultimately satisfied by unconditional Love, then could the Creator of this desire be anything less than Unconditional Love?* If we assume that the Creator did not intend to frustrate this desire for unconditional Love within all of us, it would seem that His very intention to fulfill it would indicate the presence of this quality within Him. This would mean that the Creator of the desire for unconditional Love is (as the only possible fulfillment of that desire) Himself Unconditional Love.

Here, we are only affirming the inconsistency of a "Creator incapable of unconditional Love" creating a being with the desire for perfect and unconditional Love.

When this inconsistency is unpacked, it gives rise to a four-step argument that has been implicitly recognized since the time of Saint Augustine:

a. If human beings have a desire for unconditional Love, it could not have originated from conditioned things (like physical forces, atoms, or molecules). Therefore, our desire for unconditional Love would have had to have originated from an unconditional Source (namely, Unconditional Love Itself).

b. The unconditional Source of this desire for unconditional Love would Itself have to be capable of unconditional Love (and therefore could not be limited to acts of conditioned love).

c. If the Creator of our unconditionally loving nature is truly capable of unconditional Love, then He would not have created us with this unconditionally loving nature only to frustrate it (for this would contradict the nature of unconditional Love).

d. Therefore, the unconditionally loving Creator of our desire for unconditional Love intends to fulfill that desire unconditionally.

The ramifications of this conclusion are so many that you may want to take a moment to "contemplate" on what it means for your life and destiny before we proceed to the next question.

5. *If the Creator is Unconditional Love, would He want to enter into a relationship with us of intense empathy, that is, would He want to be Emmanuel ("God with us")?* If one did not assume that love is both pure positivity and the meaning of life, then the above suggestion would be preposterous. Why would God (Who is Creator and all-powerful) want to bother with creatures, let alone actually be among them and enter into empathetic relationship with them? However, in the logic of love, or, rather, in the logic of unconditional Love, such a suggestion seems quite consistent, for love is empathizing with the other and entering into a unity with that other whereby doing the good for the other is just as easy, if not easier, than doing the good for oneself. This kind of love has the non-egocentricity, humility, self-gift, deep affection, and care that would make infinite power into infinite gentleness. In other words, "Emmanuel" would be typical of an unconditionally loving God. This would characterize the way that Unconditional Love would act; not being egocentrically conscious of the infinite distance between Creator and creature, but rather being infinitely desirous of bridging this gap in a unity opening upon pure joy. It would be just like the unconditionally loving God to be "God with us." Again, you may want to take a moment to contemplate on the remarkable consequences of this affirmation, for it not only holds the key to our eternal destiny, but also to the destiny of the entire world—the entire symphony of love.

6. *If it were typical of the unconditionally loving God to want to be fully with us, then is Jesus the One?* Jesus claimed to be the

beloved Son of *Abba* with us, to bring the kingdom of *Abba* to us, and to bring us, through Himself, to *Abba*. If this claim is true, then Jesus is Emmanuel, and our hope in God coming to be with us has been fulfilled. We do not have to bridge the infinite gap between "our desire for the unconditional" and "the unconditional actuality" by ourselves. Jesus, our Emmanuel, has come.

The affirmation of Jesus as Emmanuel lies at the center of Saint Ignatius' Spiritual Exercises. Indeed, he spends the second, third, and fourth weeks of the Exercises not only affirming this truth of all truths but also leading the person making the Exercise to love the Giver of this truth and love. I have completed a manuscript on the philosophical and scriptural evidence for this affirmation entitled *Emmanuel: Evidence of the Unconditional Love of God and the Divinity of Jesus*, and so I do not intend here to go into detail on the same subject. Nevertheless, I will present a few areas of contemplation that might help you to affirm what the early witnesses, the Scriptures, and the Holy Spirit have been proclaiming for centuries:

a. *The Holy Spirit.* Consider that the Holy Spirit, Who is incredibly active in millions of faith communities throughout the world, was proclaimed by the early Church to be the power of God through charismatic and interior manifestations of power, wisdom, and love (see chapters 4 and 5). Consider also that Jesus is the definitive giver of the Holy Spirit (the power of God). Finally, ask yourself, who but God Himself can give away the "power of God"?

b. *Resurrection.* Consider Saint Paul's reasoning for why he would not be lying about the Resurrection (presented in

1 Cor 15). Notice his dilemma: (1) If he had *not* witnessed the risen Jesus, and he *maintained faith* in the God of his forefathers, then he would have emerged as "misrepresenting God" and "of all men most to be pitied" (vv. 15 and 19). (2) Alternatively, if he had *not* witnessed the risen Jesus and did *not* have faith in God, then why not "eat and drink, for tomorrow we die" (v. 32) because "our preaching is in vain and your faith in vain" (v. 14)? Consider the fact that Saint Paul, by his own reckoning, had everything to lose and nothing to gain by preaching Jesus risen from the dead if it were not true. Consider also that all of the other early witnesses had nothing to gain and everything to lose if their testimony to the risen Jesus were false. Paul gives us his list:

> [First] he appeared to Cephas [Peter], then to the Twelve. Then he appeared to more than five hundred brethren at one time, most of whom are still alive, though some have fallen asleep. Then he appeared to James, then to all the apostles. Last of all, as to one untimely born, he appeared also to me. (vv. 5–8)

c. *The miracles of Jesus.* Consider that Jesus' miracles are attested to multiple times in all the Gospels, many of the epistles, and even in non-Christian historical sources. Consider further that His miracles are quite unique in the history of religions, because:

- Jesus does miracles by His own authority;

- Jesus' miracles have the purpose, not of showing His glory, but of actualizing the coming of the kingdom and the vanquishing of evil;

- Jesus is not a wonder worker in either the pagan or Jewish sense;

- Jesus combines teaching and miracle; and

- the faith/freedom of the recipient is integral to Jesus' miraculous deeds (see Brown 1994).

Consider, then, that the primary purpose of Jesus' miracles is not to testify to His divine power during the ministry, but, rather, to heal people in need, and through this, to bring about the reality of the kingdom of God and to vanquish evil (which also *happens* to be a demonstration of His supernatural power during His ministry). Consider further that the divine glory manifest in these miracles links Jesus' preresurrection state to the evident divine glory of His postresurrection state—light, glory, and spiritual "body" (see Saint Paul's description in 1 Cor 15).

 d. *Jesus' preaching of love.* Recall some crucial points made in the introduction to the book (which bear repeating here):

- Jesus taught us to address God as *Abba*. This address was, for the people of His time, too familiar for God, too presumptuous for the Master of the Universe, and so Jesus seems to be the first to have uttered it. Yet, when He did so, He made it the center of His theology and the basis for His identity as "Beloved Son."

- The prodigal son parable represents Jesus' consummate revelation of who *Abba* is. As shown in chapter 7 (section VII), Jesus reveals the Father to be Unconditional Love and completely trustworthy of our unconditional hope when we need forgiveness, reconciliation, and healing.

Consider two other points central to Jesus' preaching:

- That Jesus proclaims love to be the highest commandment, then links the love of God to the love of neighbor, and then proclaims that all the other commandments depend on this. Thus, love is the only commandment (virtue) that can stand on its own, and any virtue that does not lead toward love (as its end) could not be virtuous. Consider that courage apart from love could undermine individuals and the common good, so could self-discipline and every other virtue that is not oriented toward love as its proper end. Consider for a moment that in first-century Jewish culture, the Law (Torah) is reflective of the heart of God, and therefore that Jesus' proclamation of love as the highest commandment must reflect the very essence of God's heart. Consider then that Jesus knew very well that it was one and the same thing to say that "love is the highest commandment" and that "God is Love."

- Consider that the Beatitudes reflect Jesus' definition of love. Recall what was said earlier in chapter 3, namely, that love is being humble-hearted (poor in spirit) and gentle-hearted (meek); hungering for God's optimally good, loving, and salvific will (holiness); being forgiving and merciful; being pure of heart; and being peacemakers. Consider further that if love is Jesus' highest commandment, and is therefore reflective of the very nature of God, then God must be perfect and unconditional humble-heartedness, gentle-heartedness, holiness, forgiveness, mercy, purity of heart, and peacemaking. If this is Jesus' revelation of who God is, would not Jesus be Emmanuel by His own definition?

e. *Jesus' acts of love.* Jesus brings the love of His miracles to fruition in His self-sacrificial death and in the Holy Eucharist. Recall for a moment what was said earlier in chapter 1 about the Holy Eucharist. Knowing that the religious authorities sought to persecute Him, Jesus set His face resolutely toward Jerusalem because He had a plan, a plan to give Himself totally through His self-sacrificial death, communicated to future generations in the Eucharist. Inasmuch as love is "gift of self," He planned to not only give Himself but His unconditional Love to all future generations. In the gift of His blood He becomes our scapegoat, our paschal lamb, and the blood guaranteeing the covenant of eternal life. Consider that He gave Himself over to death to take the place of a sacrificial animal in actualizing unconditional Love in His very person so that the new covenant would not only forgive sins, but bring eternal life to all who accepted it. Is this something that Emmanuel would do? Would this be typical of Emmanuel? Does Jesus exemplify the "unconditional Love of God with us" in His self-sacrificial death and in His eucharistic action? Is Jesus the One?

In my faith, I simply cannot deny this. If God is Unconditional Love, and it would be typical of Unconditional Love to be with us, then the One who not only gave us the Holy Spirit, risen glory, and His miracles, but also showed us that love is the highest commandment (defining it through the Beatitudes), and then gave us that love concretely in a self-sacrificial act bestowed on all future generations through the Eucharist, would seem irresistibly to be the One. And then the Holy Spirit comes and confirms it. How could I say "no"?

IV. The Presence and Guidance of the Holy Spirit in Our Lives

The love and beauty of Jesus culminates in His gift of the Holy Spirit to lead us evermore deeply into the heart He revealed in His Passion and Eucharist. He intended that every grace be specifically tailored for optimal effects in our individual and collective lives. Much of this has been taken up in chapters 4 and 5, so, for the moment, we need only discuss the final point in Saint Ignatius' "Contemplation on Divine Love," namely, spiritual autobiography. How has the Holy Spirit been working in our hearts and in our lives to protect us, to keep us on the right road, to deepen us in our faith, and to lead us more deeply into the unconditionally loving heart of Christ and His Father? This aspect of contemplation entails writing our own gospel—the "good news of God in us."

I began this exercise as a Jesuit novice during my first long retreat, and I have been adding to it ever since. The objective of the exercise is not to write a complete history of the self (whew!), but, rather, to write a brief sacred history of how the Holy Spirit has worked through a variety of people, circumstances, joys, sufferings, talents, deficits, successes, and failures in our lives. In my life, I can identify points at which the Spirit deepened my love for Christ in my childhood, adolescence, collegiate years, and in the many stages of my Jesuit life. I will recount a few of these here so that you might get some ideas on what to look for in writing your own spiritual autobiography.

I can remember well many genuine religious experiences in my childhood—the stained glass windows at Sacred Heart Church on Wilder Avenue in Honolulu; looking at the crèche set in my home at Christmastime; my family prayers at night; my little prayer book, which I treated with great reverence during and after Mass; the way I went to sleep (most nights) with the sense that Christ was all around me. All these experiences had a similar tone or theme that seemed to be woven throughout, namely, a sense of home; a spiritual Home; a delight-filled, majestic, loving sense of being at home in the totality—at home with God.

When I was a child I did not reflectively understand what I was experiencing, and I certainly was not able to articulate it in the manner mentioned earlier concerning "spiritual con- solation" or "affective consolation." Nevertheless, I did feel at home with God, and with the heart of a child I accepted His gift of Himself to me. I took it, I believed in it, I fell asleep with it, I awoke with it; and I loved Him. Then came adolescence.

My adolescence was not a complete loss, but it did have challenges. I can honestly say that I did not lose my interest in God at the age of thirteen, but I did begin to experience the uncertainties intrinsic to a myriad of questions. Fellow students would be talking about the existence of God, some even had a vague awareness of Sartre and Nietzsche, and others an acute awareness of the seeming incompatibility of suffering and a loving God. I had a particularly good friend who believed I would have some deeper answer to these questions and so constantly besieged me with questions such as "Why would God allow us to suffer?" "Why did He allow evil in the world?" "Why did He allow the concentration camps to happen?" I kept telling him, "I can't answer all your questions, because you will always find some response that will make my answer look stupid. But I do know this. . . . God has a plan, and that plan is bigger than I will ever be able to comprehend. If I could see how God acted in the hearts of every human being and how He was trying to lead us all *together* into His kingdom, then I could give you specific answers to all your questions—including the one about the concentration camps." My friend found this a particularly unsatisfying answer, and, unfortunately, I think my faith seemed to drive him further away from me. But eventually he would always come back for one more try to see if I could give him a more specific answer. I was amazed by the fact that I believed my answer. I seemed to know with *certainty* what caused *him* so much doubt. I recognized that I did not have adequate rational grounding for my certainty, but nevertheless I had a deep authentic sense that what I said and what I meant was true. Though I did not at the time recognize this as the inspiration of the Holy Spirit (*sensus fidei*), it did cause me to think that my faith was not only real, but would be one of the most important aspects of my life.

Throughout this time I began to reflect deeply on the evidence for God. I read various catechisms, investigated exciting new scientific prospects in Big Bang cosmology (which was at its infancy in 1968), probed more deeply into the problem of suffering, and thought about my relationship to God. The more I was challenged, the more my interest in God intensified, and the more I began to probe deeply into theological questions. I was completely unaware of the many theological treatises that dealt with these subjects because they were not presented to me either in school or in catechism class.

During this time, the Church became the center point of my faith. Even though I was trying to answer questions about the existence of God from the vantage point of quasi-philosophical and physical evidence, the *Church* held me to the truth of faith. My philosophical musings did not respond to my inquiries about the meaning of suffering, but, rather, I found answers in the Good Friday liturgy and the beautiful crucifix in our church. My reading and writing about the meaning of life (even from the vantage point of faith) was not persuasive by itself. It needed to be supported by the Mass—with its prayers, its contrition and forgiveness, its Gospel and sermon, its transcendent symbolism, its beauty, and, above all, the Eucharist, which together evoked a sense of Home. I was at home in the Church, and that sense of Home kept me faithful to what I would later know to be perfect Intelligibility, Goodness, and Love.

Then came Gonzaga University. This was one of the most positive periods in my life because so many things occurred to deepen my faith intellectually, morally, and spiritually. My friends and many of my professors were clearly a gift from God, so also were the books I read, the Masses in which I participated, and the discussions I had with colleagues and adversaries alike. The richness of this period precludes my writing a holistic account of it, for it would be too long and arduous to benefit readers who may be looking solely for hints on how to construct their own spiritual history. Therefore, I will restrict myself to a brief account of several experiences of grace (the loving action of the Holy Spirit) that drew me closer to God and His call to the Society of Jesus.

In the second semester of my sophomore year, when I was still trying to bolster my faith with rational justification, I "happened" to pass by a metaphysics class. I overheard the professor speaking about a particular proof for the existence of God. I was absolutely dumbfounded by the prospect, thinking, "*Hey, you can't prove the existence of God.*" So I slipped into the back of the classroom and began to listen to his explanation. I thoroughly enjoyed logic, so the rigor of the proof delighted and fascinated me. After the class, I went up to the professor and said, "Well, I follow your logic thus far, but I still don't think you can prove the existence of God." The professor said, "Well, are you saying this as a matter of principle or because you intend to criticize my particular proof?" "*Gulp,*" I thought. "*I think I just tried to* aprioristically *deny the possibility of* aprioristically *affirming the existence of God.*" I related this to the professor, who readily agreed that I was doing precisely that. He invited me to attend the whole metaphysics class in the next semester, which I did.

This class opened up a whole domain of discourse, which I found to be quite liberating. To think about ultimacy in causation, grounds of existence, being; indeed, to think about causation itself, space, time, unity; to think about the transcendentals (Truth, Love, Goodness, Beauty, and Being Itself) was absolutely astonishing to me. Even if one were to think about such things only to criticize them, the thoughts themselves were ennobling. They were the highest viewpoints to which the human mind could aspire; and they seemed to hold the key to the analysis of everything from quantum systems, to the fundamental insights of mathematics, to the underlying insight of logic itself, and, indeed, to the ground of onto-logic, that is, God. So began the road to my progressive realization of the remarkable rational evidence for the existence of God.

Some might say that it was a "happy coincidence" that I was passing by a metaphysics class that day at the precise time the professor was saying "… proof for the existence of God." Perhaps it was, but even so, the inspiration that took place through that chance or graced occurrence that ennobled my spirit, that revealed the grounds of thought itself—that inspiration for me, like Augustine, had to be attributed to the Holy Spirit.

In the second semester of my junior year, a girl to whom I was favorably attracted said to me, "Spitzer, you ought to go on a Search retreat." I indicated to her that I much preferred public accounting, finance, math, and so forth, and I really wasn't the "retreat type." She was truly disappointed and even accused me of being affectively retarded if not heartless; this got me to thinking, *"Maybe I don't have much of a heart— maybe I ought to do some work on that."* So I relented and let her talk me into it. Without revealing how the retreat opened my heart, I will simply say this—the combination of prayer, the interaction with others, a movie on Mother Teresa, and a letter from my parents had the remarkable effect of short-circuiting my desire to analyze the entire experience. The impact of the stimulus of love manifest so acutely in that weekend managed to do two things: (1) it allowed me to accept the *reality* of love for me rather than the *concept* of "love"; and (2) it allowed me to intuit the love of God in that experience of love. These two experiences were major "breakthroughs of the heart," and they led to a progressive opening of my heart not only to the importance, but also the primacy of love—the love of God in Jesus Christ.

Shortly after my Search experience, another girl to whom I was also favorably attracted said to me, "We need someone to teach ninth-and tenth-grade catechism class." I retorted that I could do public accounting, finance, or math, but not catechism class. She said, "Well, you seem to know a lot about your faith and you go to Mass often . . . so I thought you might be able to share something with the students." I said that I would really prefer not to, at which point she looked crestfallen. In an effort to "excuse my way out of it," I noted, "Well, the only thing I really know about are proofs for the existence of God and some indications of creation from Big Bang cosmology." She said, "That will be fine." So I was stuck.

I went to my first catechism class and started talking about proofs for the existence of God and indications of creation in Big Bang cosmology. To my great surprise, the students were utterly fascinated. They told me that it was the best catechism class they had ever had and that they were all going to come back the next week so that they could hear more about it. To top matters off, they told the girl who got me into the fix in the first place. She rushed up to me on Monday morning and told me how popular the class had been, and then said, "Surely you won't turn them down. I'm sure you're going to teach the next class, and perhaps a few more." I could not refuse her. Indeed, I thought, *"If I don't teach these students, God might justifiably be stunned at my hardness of heart."* So I agreed, and I began to love the students, to love enlightening them about the goodness and beauty and being of God, and, as a result, to love teaching. I became so hooked on those crazy kids that I actually told the girl, "I like teaching so much, I could make it a career." That was a prophecy. Though

I continued on my public accounting and finance track, I began to audit as many philosophy and theology courses as I could. I volunteered to teach catechism whenever needed, and I became strangely drawn not only to the philosophical and theological enterprise, but to the passionate elucidation of the Truth, Goodness, Love, and Beauty that had become the center of my life.

One could call this incident a "happy coincidence," but I cannot help but think that the girl who invited me to teach was an agent of the Holy Spirit. What did she see in a "quant" like me? Why did she invite *me* to teach the class rather than somebody else? Why was she so adamant? I had occasion to ask her about three years ago when I ran into her at a Gonzaga alumni function, and she told me, "I don't really know. I think I was just inspired." I knew it!

The reader may now want to return to chapter 4 (section IV) to correlate the events in these stories with the pattern of the Holy Spirit's inspiration and guidance. Recall that the Holy Spirit's favorite tactic is to draw us into an opportunity, then open doors into that opportunity, then draw us further into the opportunity through a sense of peace, excitement, and zeal, and then open more doors, etc.

Toward the end of my senior year, I was cascading toward a priestly vocation. One of the Jesuit professors whose course I was auditing invited me to participate in a three-day version of the Spiritual Exercises. I do not know why I said yes so readily to a silent retreat, but I did. I was very excited about it though I did not know why. As I entered into the retreat, I began to experience spiritual consolation in a very deep way. God's signature impression (a synthesis of the feelings of "home amid the totality," mystery, ultimacy, love, joy, beauty, and awe) seemed to grow in intensity as I walked along the trails of the Bozarth retreat house, as I read the Scriptures, as I thought about my life, and as I participated in the Holy Eucharist. I was captivated, drawn, loved outside of myself. God had brought me to a crossroads, and He was strongly inviting me to come further.

An odd thing happened at that point. I told the retreat director that I thought I might want to become a Jesuit. I really hadn't thought about that previously. It kind of blurted out of my mouth. I think I was shocked to hear myself say it. He recognized that I was in a state of consolation and wisely counseled me to think about it over the next several weeks to see if my thoughts would strengthen or weaken, whether it was merely the fervor of the retreat or the fervor of a call. The consolation remained and this required a visit to the novitiate and its paint room (recounted in the previous chapter). The rest is history—or should I say, providence.

The above autobiographical passages were meant to illustrate how one might go about writing a spiritual autobiography. The key is to ask for the inspiration of the Holy Spirit and to jot down notes about childhood religious experiences; adolescent challenges; little or great turning points in your life; general momentums of deepening awareness of faith, hope, or love; sufferings that have led to deeper meaning, faith, love, or positive life changes; consolations that manifest the loving presence of God; God working through influential people and "difficult people"; etc. Be sensitive to the subtlety of providence. And, above all, be appreciative of the love that has been showered down upon you. It will open upon a greater love.

This was Saint Ignatius' intention in writing the "Contemplation on Divine Love." When one contemplatively considers the wonders of creation, the even greater wonder of our transcendental soul, the unconditional Love of Jesus' redemptive act, and the personal care of the Holy Spirit through the stages on life's way, one cannot help but be impressed. One cannot help but say, "Thank You," and in the mere thanking, in the mere praise of the loving God, the Holy Spirit opens our hearts to yet a deeper stage of humility, gentleness, holiness, forgiveness, mercy, purity of heart, and peacemaking. Oddly enough, the recipe for entering more deeply into the Beatitudes is not a stoic resolve. It is not an assertion from within the self that says, "I am now going to be more humble-hearted, and I have constructed a four-stage plan to get there." It comes, rather, from an awareness of the love of God for creation, humanity, and our personal selves that causes us to say, "Thank You," and, "God be praised." Then, with the slightest effort, the Holy Spirit can nudge us into what we cannot give ourselves. As peculiar as it may seem, this is the path to true freedom, freedom toward the unconditional Love of God.

Chapter Seven

Fifth Pillar: The Contemplative Life (*Continued*)— Ignatian Contemplation on the Heart of Jesus

Introduction

The essence of Ignatian contemplation is to put ourselves into a scene with Jesus and to enter into the actions and discourse of Jesus with His disciples, so that He might speak to us as He spoke to them and that we might see His love as His disciples saw it. If you believe that Jesus is the One, that He is Emmanuel, the Unconditional Love of God with us; that He has redeemed us by His blood, loved us into salvation, and gives us an eternal life of love and joy through our mere belief in His loving and forgiving heart; then it is now time to probe that heart more deeply through various Gospel scenes, where we can see His love for His disciples manifest in their love and trust of Him.

Normally, you would make these contemplations on a retreat where separation, silence, and a director would allow you to deepen "the lessons of the heart" within these meditations. I offer them to you here so that you might be able to get a partial idea about what Ignatian contemplation can reveal. If you have occasion to go on a retreat, you may want to take this book with you and review the contents of this and the previous chapter as your retreat director might see fit. My point here is that these meditations are merely the tip of the iceberg.

I. The Wedding Feast at Cana (Jn 2:1–11)

Jesus accompanies His mother and disciples to a wedding feast in Cana. During the feast the host runs out of wine, which would have led to his being humiliated for his lack of forethought and hospitality. Jesus' mother hears about it and is moved to help the host. She asks Jesus to help him, confident that Jesus can do something (either naturally or supernaturally). Jesus is reticent because His "hour has not yet come." He was not yet prepared to perform a deed of power (a miracle) because He associated these deeds with the vanquishing of evil and the bringing of the kingdom of heaven (the hallmarks of His ministry, which he had not yet begun).

What is quite remarkable here is that Jesus' mother will not accept no for an answer. Instead of discussing the matter any further, she turns to the wine steward with complete confidence and says, "Do whatever he tells you." Needless to say, she has not only defied her son's wishes, but also "put Him on the spot" in front of the steward and the host.

Two aspects of this exchange are important. First, Jesus, fully aware of the power of the Spirit, which He is about to use, and therefore fully aware of His special relationship to the Father, takes His mother's response completely in stride (with apparent humility). He manifests no anger, resentment, hurt, inconvenience, or specialness, and allows His love and respect for His mother to override His plan for salvation. Though He did not have to jeopardize the plan to accommodate His mother, He did have to redraw a multitude of lines. The second striking feature is the seeming "unimportance" of the miracle. Jesus here is not healing someone crippled or blind from birth, raising someone from the dead, casting out a demon, or bringing the kingdom in His own person. His first miracle, according to John, is helping a host at a party with a "wine problem." In combining these two features, I cannot help but reflect on Jesus' phrase "for I am gentle (*prais*) and humble (*tapeinos*) in heart. . . . My yoke is easy, and my burden is light" (Mt 11:29–30, author's translation). Mary's confidence in her son, her trust in His response, and her awareness that her request (no matter how inconsequential it might be in the whole order of salvation) would be respected, reveals *her intimate* knowledge of her son's heart. Through Mary's eyes, nothing is too little or inconsequential for her son, and she trusts completely in His love and respectfulness.

Now we begin to see the meaning of Jesus' final commandment in John: "Love one another as I have loved you." Jesus' love extends to little people in little circumstances with seemingly little problems (in the order of salvation). His love is humble and gentle and abides inconvenience and modification of plans. It engenders at once affection, trust, and hope. Would Emmanuel (the Unconditional Love of God with us) be like this? Could He be other than this? Now, put yourself in the scene and let it unfold as the Holy Spirit directs.

II. The Call of Nathanael (Jn 1:43–50)

After Jesus has called Peter, his brother Andrew, and Philip, Philip finds Nathanael and reports to him with an enthusiasm that Nathanael (probably by personality) is reticent to share: "We have found him of whom Moses in the law and also the prophets wrote, Jesus of Nazareth, the son of Joseph." One can feel in the response of Nathanael a bit of his personality. He probably sees himself as a "realist" (perhaps even a skeptic) who can spot the error in Philip's statement immediately (the Messiah was supposed to come from the city of David—not Nazareth in Galilee). But Nathanael also has an edge to his personality and cannot help insulting both Philip and the town from which Jesus came: "Can anything good come out of Nazareth?" Nevertheless, Philip prevails and takes Nathanael to meet Jesus.

Jesus' reaction to Nathanael is quite interesting. When He sees him coming, He (with tongue somewhat buried in cheek) says to him, "Behold, an Israelite indeed, in whom [there] is no guile!" Nathanael is, to say the least, a bit surprised at Jesus' extraordinarily perceptive remark. After all, he is a realist (perhaps a bit skeptical); he tells it like it is, and with a bit of an edge. He queries back to Jesus, "How do you know me?"

Instead of telling Nathanael straight on, Jesus decides to let "the realist" figure it out for himself and reveals to Nathanael something that no normal person could have known about him: "Before Philip called you, when you were under the fig tree, I saw you." The "realist" does not disappoint Jesus. He blurts out a veritable confession of faith almost immediately: "Rabbi, you are the Son of God! You are the King of Israel!" Jesus, not wishing to waste the revelatory moment, decides to keep "the realist" engaged and to point out that he is exemplifying enthusiasms similar to the ones he disdained in Philip: "Because I said to you, I saw you under the fig tree, do you believe? You shall see greater things than these. . . . Truly,

truly, I say to you, you will see heaven opened, and the angels of God ascending and descending upon the Son of man."

Two points may be gleaned from this call. First, Jesus needs some "edgy realists" in His company and has no intention of turning Nathanael into another personality type who might be more genteel or better suited to proper company. He accepts Nathanael precisely "where he is." Jesus seems to like a wide variety of personality types (including the edgy ones) and responds to Nathanael's insults with a quasi-compliment: "An Israelite . . . in whom [there] is no guile." He uses Nathanael's powers of insight to elicit a confession of faith. Obviously, Jesus has heard Nathanael's insults, but is completely unconcerned about them. He is concerned about Nathanael and is concerned to call him in a way that will move him to deep faith and apostolic service.

Secondly, Jesus allows Nathanael to be free throughout his call. He allows Philip to find Nathanael, allows Nathanael to insult His hometown, provokes him with an enticing clue to His powers, allows him to respond to that clue, and then, after Nathanael's confession, reveals the full truth about Himself. Is such a method commensurate with love? Would love be any other way? Would Emmanuel be this accepting? Would He use enticing clues and "tongue in cheek" expressions and wait for the free response? Now, put yourself in the scene and let it unfold as the Holy Spirit directs.

III. The Samaritan Woman (Jn 4:1–29)

Jesus and His disciples arrive in a Samaritan town. (Some Samaritans feel resentment toward perceived Jewish superiority.) They go to an important historical religious site (Jacob's

Well). Jesus' disciples go to town for supplies, leaving Him alone by the well. After a while, a woman comes up with her buckets to collect water from the well, and Jesus, seeing a "target of inestimable opportunity," decides to engage her. The woman is considerably more edgy than Nathanael, and she has a bit of a sarcastic streak. The sarcasm may be a feature of her personality, but it may also be attributable to a state of life that is not altogether laudable (she has had five husbands). Her neighbors probably know about this, which adds to the hard exterior that she so easily manifests. As far as she knows, Jesus is a total stranger.

As she approaches the well, Jesus asks her for a drink of water. Seeing that Jesus does not have a bucket, and knowing she has an advantage over Him, she decides to seize the irresistible chance to get back at "His people" for their perceived superiority: "How is it that you, a Jew, ask a drink of me, a woman of Samaria?" She believes she has Jesus "over a barrel" because if He says He would like a drink anyway, He would be in an awkward, if not embarrassing, position; and if He says, "Oh, that's okay—forget it," He goes thirsty at noon (the sixth Jewish hour), one of the hottest parts of the day.

Jesus decides to avoid the dilemma by elevating the discussion to what *He* can give the woman: "If you knew the gift of God, and who it is that is saying to you, 'Give me a drink,' you would have asked him and he would have given you living water." The woman finds this "elevated remark" incomprehensible and humorous and retorts sarcastically, "Sir, you have nothing to draw with, and the well is deep; where do you get that living water? Are you greater than our father Jacob, who gave us the well, and drank from it himself, and his sons, and his cattle?" Little does the woman know how ironically correct her inquiry is and how it plays into Jesus' hand. So He continues to offer her the gift of life: "Every one who drinks of this water will thirst again, but whoever drinks of the water that I shall give him will never thirst. The water that I shall give him will become in him a spring of water welling up to eternal life." The woman cannot resist the impulse to let Jesus have it with her most demeaning comment yet: "Sir, give me this water, that I may not thirst, nor come here to draw."

Jesus does not mind the belittling remark, yet since He wants to draw the woman to new life, He makes a request: "Go, call your husband, and come here." She replies that she has no husband. Jesus knows her lie, but does not accuse her of it. Instead, He acknowledges what little truth there is in the statement by noting, "You are right in saying, 'I have no husband'; for you have had five husbands, and he whom you now have is not your husband; this you said truly." The woman, recognizing that she is in a bind, blurts out the obvious, "Sir, I perceive that you are a prophet."

It is interesting that the woman does not walk off (either defensively or aggressively). She is taken (not merely intrigued) by Jesus' prophetic state and actually starts engaging Him in theological discourse. Despite her state of life, matters of religion did make a difference to her, and Jesus seems to have seized upon it. Instead of lecturing her about her misdeeds, He speaks to her about matters of messiahship, spiritual worship, and other very elevated matters (dignifying her instead of demeaning her).

After hearing Jesus' discourse, the woman begins to wonder whether Jesus might be the Messiah, and so she probes Him: "I know that [the] Messiah is coming. . . . [W]hen he comes, he will show us all things." Jesus then makes an extraordinary revelation: "I who speak to you am he." The transformation of the woman's attitude through Jesus' gentle, dignifying, and merciful manner is simply extraordinary. She literally becomes His first disciple to the foreign lands and goes back to her town saying, "Come, see a man who told me all that I ever did. Can this be the Christ?"

Notice Jesus' tactics here. He does not compel or push, but rather appeals to the woman's religious interests and elicits continually deepening, *free* responses: first a prophet, then possibly the Messiah, then the Messiah. Even though Jesus turns the conversation by making a provocative request, He gives her a wide berth to respond. She could have walked off, but instead she chose to lie. Jesus could have chastised her for the lie, but instead He acknowledges the truth within it. Again, the woman could have walked off, but instead she chooses to acknowledge Him as a prophet and, after listening to His discourse, is so excited that she actually probes Him as to whether He is the Messiah. Jesus has her hooked.

After returning to the town, she invites everyone to come and see Jesus. Apparently, she is quite convincing because a considerable number make their way over to Jacob's Well. Note that Jesus is only too happy to oblige the woman's missionary impulses and is unconcerned with her being foreign, a woman, and a person with a "less than stellar" reputation. Her missionary activity provides the occasion for Jesus to stay in the town for two days, at their invitation! This, in turn, enables Him to bring others to belief in His messiahship (His being "Savior of the world"). The woman could have left Jesus and went back to her "former life," but she obviously felt reconciled, healed, and grateful and was filled with a spiritual enthusiasm that initiated a great missionary good.

Would Emmanuel have a manner similar to Jesus'? Would He allow such disciples in His company? Would He bestow such spiritual blessings through someone like this? Now, put yourself in the scene and let it unfold as the Holy Spirit directs.

IV. A Collage of Peter

There are so many revelations about the love of Jesus manifested through Peter in the Gospels that it might be best to present a collage of passages giving insight into the trust and love of this disciple for Jesus.

Peter is an interesting mixture of character traits that Jesus finds essential for his forthcoming mission and leadership. In my view, the most important of these is his childlike trust in Jesus opening upon apostolic zeal and a desire to be a companion of Jesus. All of these characteristics galvanize Peter's love. A few stories will help to concretize this remarkable personality.

Peter's childlike heart is manifested in his spontaneity. This can be clearly gleaned from the synoptic Gospels where Peter (at the Transfiguration—in what must have seemed to be a resplendent revelation of Jesus' transcendent glory, which would have provoked most people to reverence and awe) says almost innocently and intimately to Jesus, "Master, it is well that we are here; let us make three booths, one for you and one for Moses and one for Elijah." The narrator is so dumbfounded by this he notes, "not knowing what he said" (Lk 9:33). Again, we can detect Peter's childlike devotion to Jesus when Jesus asks, after being rejected, "Will you also go away?" And Peter turns to Him in faith, trust, and devotion, and says, "Lord, to whom shall we go? You have the words of eternal life" (Jn 6:67–68).

In Matthew's Gospel when Peter sees Jesus walking on water (see Mt 14:25–33), he manifests a remarkable childlike calm and curiosity, saying, "Lord, if it is you, bid me come to you on the water." Even though this story is intended to be an epiphany (revelatory of the divinity of Christ with postresurrection implications), it manages, amidst this divine glory, to reveal Peter's childlike heart. As at the Transfiguration, when Peter sees Jesus he is not caught up in awe, but rather wants to come out onto the water too. Jesus says, "Come." And with the trust and heart of a child, Peter gets out of the boat and walks toward Jesus. He then (somewhat late) figures out that he might be in a precarious situation and begins to drown. Again, with the heart of a child and the seriousness of an adult he exclaims, "Lord, save me!" and Jesus does.

John's Gospel complements these and other synoptic accounts with other examples of Peter's trust, devotion, and love. When Jesus is at table with the apostles prior to His Passion, He readies Himself to wash their feet (see Jn 13:1–15). Peter's devotion to Jesus is so profound that he cannot imagine Jesus doing for him what would ordinarily be done by a servant boy, and so he exclaims, "You shall never wash my feet." Peter means this in the best possible way, namely, that he is not deserving of such a self-deprecating act by his Lord and Master. Jesus says to him, "If I do not wash you, you have no part in me." Jesus is doing this in order to reveal His loving nature and to provide an example for His disciples to do likewise; but Peter does not yet understand. Nevertheless, he puts his trust completely in Jesus and then, with the spontaneity and exaggerated impulse of a child, says, "Lord, not my feet only but also my hands and my head!" Jesus calms Peter's enthusiasm and proceeds with His instruction. It is interesting to note that Jesus seems to value Peter's childlike heart as much as His traditional leadership qualities and loyalty.

Jesus' resurrection appearance at the Sea of Tiberias is very revealing of Jesus' heart (see Jn 21:1–25). The story begins with Peter exemplifying *traditional* leadership qualities. He says, "I am going fishing," to which the others respond, "We will go with you." One can sense Peter taking the lead in the boat, casting the nets into the sea all night, but catching nothing. When Jesus appears on the shore (unrecognized by the disciples), He asks, "Children, have you any fish?" and they answer, "No." The stranger advises them that if they cast their nets over the starboard side they will catch something. Indeed, they do: a miraculous draught. John (the more quiet, contemplative, and perceptive disciple) recognizes Jesus and informs Peter, "It is the Lord!" (using the definite article in front of "Lord," indicating a postresurrection manifestation of divinity). Peter once again springs into childlike action with an overwhelming joy and enthusiasm (reminiscent of children seeing their parents come back from a long trip). He jumps into the water and swims ashore to be with Jesus (leaving the disciples behind in the boat with the fish). One can sense Peter's joy amidst his trust.

Recall that Peter had denied Jesus three times, and that these denials were as yet unreconciled. Peter does not seem to be worried in the least about how Jesus will greet him (when he is diving into the water). He is not worried about Jesus feeling angry, betrayed, hurt, dismayed; all he seems to care about is that Jesus is back and he is overwhelmingly happy to see Him. It is obvious that Peter trusts Jesus, but notice how he trusts Him—by instinctively knowing Jesus' heart. This awareness of Jesus' love for him causes his joy to overwhelm any residual fear or remorse that he might feel. Peter has years of experience of Jesus' love and acceptance, compounded by a sense that Jesus can reconcile and renew even the most egregious of offenses. It is this childlike knowledge of being beloved, cared for, accepted, reconciled, and rekindled that causes him to completely trust Jesus and to enthusiastically greet Him amidst the tumult of the events of the Passion.

Jesus lives up to Peter's trust. He has a charcoal fire ready and makes them breakfast. Afterward, He takes Peter aside and combines an act of reconciliation (presumably for Peter's three denials) with an act of missioning through a simple question: "Simon, son of John, do you love me more than these? . . . Feed my lambs." In the following two verses Jesus asks Peter a second and third time to "tend" and "feed" His "sheep." Peter's response to Jesus' queries completes the rite of reconciliation, which is done far more for Peter than for Jesus. It is important for *Peter* to know that Jesus has heard him say, "Lord, you know everything; you know that I love you." Each confession of love (act of reconciliation) enables Jesus to entrust His mission to Peter in a primary way.

The use of "sheep" and "lambs" is significant because they manifest such incredible need and vulnerability. Jesus loves His needy and vulnerable ones and shows His trust and love of Peter by entrusting his most precious beloveds to him. *Agape* is the operative activity here. Jesus has loved and cared for Peter so deeply that Peter has a deep intuitive awareness of His heart. This intuitive awareness leads Peter to a childlike trust and love of his Master and Lord, which, in turn, has led Jesus to a trust in Peter's ability to feed and tend (and love in the imitation of Jesus) His most precious beloveds.

Here we get a glimpse of the concrete meaning of Jesus' commandment to love in the Gospel of John: "As the Father has loved me, so have I loved you; abide in my love.... This is my commandment, that you love one another as I have loved you" (Jn 15:9, 12). Inasmuch as the evangelist intended this meaning and understood the heart of Peter understanding the heart of Jesus, the depth and extent of Jesus' concrete love for Peter (and His lambs) can scarcely be doubted. Would such a love typify Emmanuel? Could Emmanuel be other than this concretely manifested open heart for Peter, for the evangelist (the "beloved disciple"), and for the world (His lambs)? If Emmanuel would be like Jesus, trust Him as Peter did. Now, put yourself in the scene and let it unfold as the Holy Spirit directs.

V. The Death of Lazarus (Jn 11:1–57)

As Jesus makes His way to Jerusalem, He goes beyond the Jordan to the place where John began his ministry of baptism. He receives word that His beloved friend Lazarus ("he whom you love") is sick. The word came from Mary and Martha, the sisters of Lazarus, who are also His beloved friends. Mary is so devoted (and presumably grateful) to Jesus that earlier she showed Him an extraordinary sign of love by anointing His feet with ointment and drying them with her hair.

Instead of going to Bethany immediately, Jesus delays for two days, indicating to His disciples that He is doing so "for the glory of God," but "this illness is not unto death." At first glance, this may seem callous or uncaring, but Jesus intends to restore Lazarus to life, making him the instrument through which the glory of God would be revealed. As yet, the disciples, the sisters, and Lazarus do not understand Jesus' plan (which He believes to be the Father's loving will, leading not only to the revelation of His love and glory, but also to the salvation of the world). Jesus' awareness of God's universal loving will is quite beyond His friends', and so they are constrained to trust Him.

First, Martha comes out to meet Jesus when He is about two miles outside of Bethany. She must have been somewhat bewildered and hurt that He delayed two days in coming, and therefore her statement, "Lord, if you had been here, my brother would not have died," expressed not merely faith in Jesus, but also that bewilderment. Apparently, Martha had a personality inclined toward strength and trust, for she is not weeping, but instead thinking ahead to what Jesus might still be able to do. So she says to Him, "even now I know that whatever you ask from God, God will give you." Jesus immediately reassures her, saying, "Your brother will rise again," to which Martha responds, "I know that he will rise again in the resurrection at the last day." It seems as if Martha is prodding Him to see if there is anything *more* than the resurrection on the last day. Jesus responds, "I am the resurrection and the life; he who believes in me, though he die, yet shall he live, and whoever lives and believes in me shall never die. Do you believe this?" At this point, Martha manifests her trust, which goes beyond her powers of understanding. She is familiar enough with Jesus to know that His statement will ultimately result in the good for Lazarus, her family, and far beyond. So she says, "Yes, Lord; I believe that you are the Christ, the Son of God, he who is coming into the world."

Notice Jesus' accessibility to Martha, and the way He allows her to affect, prod, and even wheedle Him. When Martha returns home, she informs Mary of Jesus' impending arrival, at which point Mary rushes out to meet Him. Mary is quite different than Martha and is much more inclined toward emotion and showing love. She falls at Jesus' feet (which the more rational Martha was probably not inclined to do) and overtly weeps. As He does with Martha, Jesus responds to Mary according to *her* heart. His empathy is so strong that when He sees her weeping, He becomes "deeply moved in spirit and [was] troubled." This expression indicates a deep degree of grief with Mary's grief and loss. Jesus knew the power of the Spirit within Him and knew He was about to reveal His glory, so His grief could not have been engendered by Lazarus' death alone; so what led to His afflicted and troubled spirit? The only explanation would seem to be His unconditional empathy with Martha and Mary (whom He loved). Jesus felt what Mary felt and was moved in His depths as Mary was moved in hers; and despite the fact that He was about to raise Lazarus from the dead, He could not help Himself. He loved them so transparently, indeed, unconditionally.

Jesus then asks Mary, "Where have you laid him?" and accompanies Mary and the crowd to the tomb. Upon seeing the collective sadness, Jesus is moved to weep. Then, as Jesus approaches the tomb, He is deeply moved in spirit a third time.

When Jesus approaches the front of the tomb, He asks that the stone be removed. The ever-practical Martha indicates to Him that there will surely be a stench. Jesus is undeterred. When the stone is removed, Jesus prays to the Father so that the crowd may believe that the time of His glory has arrived. This is in no way narcissistic, and Jesus explains His motives in His prayer to the Father, realizing that this act will initiate "the glory of God" by engendering a plot against His life. Jesus knows that raising Lazarus is not the source of His glory, but His impending death by crucifixion.

The event is filled with ironies: an act of love is about to engender an act of hate: "[T]he chief priests and the Pharisees gathered the council, and said, 'What are we to do? For this man performs many signs. If we let him go on like this, every one will believe in him. . . .'" Yet, the act of hate will lead to Jesus' total "gift of self" ("love") on the Cross, which love will be unconditional and universal for all time. Thus, Jesus' "glory" is not in showing off His power to the crowd—far from it. His glory comes from initiating the process that will lead Him to the Cross and His unconditional act of love (self-gift) for the world. This gives a fuller sense to the delay in going up to see Lazarus. Jesus' delay here prefigures His own time in the tomb prior to His Resurrection.

When Jesus completes His prayer, He calls Lazarus forth, clearly indicating His power over death. It is as if His word overpowers death and reanimates Lazarus. When Lazarus comes out of the tomb, Jesus commands, "Unbind him, and let him go [free]." The sense of Jesus' final command here is one of freedom or liberation. It is precisely what the Father (whom Jesus reveals to be the God of Love) desires for all of us. It is not a freedom leading to complete autonomy or "getting what one wants," but a freedom to live in the light of the children of God. The power to overcome death is the power to overcome spiritual death (not merely material death), and Jesus' glory (in the fuller sense of His impending Passion, death, and

Resurrection as an act of unconditional Love) is the means through which that freedom from spiritual death is about to occur. Unconditional Love overcomes all forms of death, and its consequence is the freedom to live as children of God.

Would Emmanuel seek any other glory than that which would occur through self-gift (*agape*)? Would He desire any other freedom for us than to become children of God (likened unto Himself)? Could Emmanuel be other than purely transparent empathy that can grieve with grief and weep in the depths of the spirit? The signs point to the spirit and love of Jesus as Emmanuel. Trust Him. Now, put yourself in the scene and let it unfold as the Holy Spirit directs.

VI. The Road to Emmaus (Lk 24:13–32)

Jesus' postresurrection appearances can be divided into two sorts: those with several witnesses (e.g., the Twelve together, five hundred of the brethren all at once, all the apostles; see 1 Cor 15:5–8; Mt 28:16–20; and Lk 24:36–52) and those with one or two witnesses (e.g., the appearance to Mary Magdalen; see Jn 20:14–18) and the appearance on the road to Emmaus (see Lk 24:13–32). Jesus' appearance to a group tends to have the features of a theophany. It is powerful, spiritual, and strikes awe and even terror, *after* which this obvious divine presence is revealed to be the crucified Jesus. There is little doubt that "*God* is appearing." The revelation is that "the appearance of God" is the crucified Jesus.

Appearances to one, two, or a *small* group of disciples are characteristically different. Jesus comes in a transformed *human* form, almost sedately (the opposite of a theophany) and tries to induce recognition through some feature of the *heart*. He induces Mary Magdalen's recognition by the pronunciation of her name (see Jn 20:16); induces some of His apostles' recognition at the Sea of Tiberias by characteristic words and signs (see Jn 21:4–8); and, in the story of the disciples on the road to Emmaus, induces recognition through His companionship, opening of the Scriptures, and finally "the breaking of the bread." We can better understand how Jesus leads us and reveals Himself to us in our everyday lives by observing carefully how He works with His disciples after the Resurrection. Normally, He uses (through the Holy Spirit) a combination of familiar signs, a sense of home, some familiar truths, the voice of the Church, and a host of little coincidences that all add up to surprising revelations about His way and truth in our lives. This is the fruit of the story of Emmaus.

Imagine Cleopas and his friend walking toward Emmaus about the middle of the morning, a few days after Jesus' crucifixion. They are discussing all that had happened to Jesus in the previous days, and what it meant to them and their future. As revealed by their admission, "We *had* hoped that he was the one to redeem Israel" (Lk 24:21), their hope is shattered, and they are trying to understand the meaning of what seems to be a senseless tragedy. Jesus (characteristically) walks up to them in a transformed human form, pretending to be a curious stranger. He asks, "What is this conversation which you are holding with each other as you walk?" The two disciples, obviously involved in their discussion, seem somewhat irked by the question and so respond, "Are you the only visitor to Jerusalem who does not know the things that have happened there in these days?" Jesus, using His usual tactics, responds, "What things?" and then lets them tell Him about everything that has happened, which includes both a testimony to their hopes for His messiahship and an admission that their hopes had been dashed.

Jesus then changes His tone from one of a friendly interlocutor to a prophetic figure. He chides them and then begins to open the Scriptures to them about what kind of person the Messiah was supposed to be. As He walks along, He not only reveals that the Messiah was not to be a "soldier liberator," but rather a self-sacrificial offering in love for humanity: "Was it not necessary that the Christ [Messiah] should suffer these things and enter into his glory?" He then begins to reveal the meaning of various prophetic sayings about the Messiah from the time of Moses until the current time. As the disciples hear the message, they become increasingly intrigued, their hopes are beginning to rekindle, and their hearts are burning within them. He has them hooked—hooked by His revelation, His presence, and the hope He offers.

As the day begins to draw on, He again uses his usual tactic and pretends that He is going farther down the road. By this time, the hearts of the two disciples are on fire, so they try to convince Him to stay with them for the night: "Stay with us, for it is toward evening and the day is now far spent." Jesus allows Himself to be invited in and seats Himself at table with the disciples. At the very moment of the breaking of the bread, the disciples recognize Him definitively. The Eucharistic symbolism, His unique presence, and the clues about His messiahship all find a nexus in a flash of insight-recognition-revelation; and when their hearts are certain, the revelation is complete and Jesus disappears from their midst.

Is this the way Emmanuel would conduct Himself? Would this be typical of incarnate, Unconditional Love? Would

Emmanuel allow us the freedom to grasp Him with our hearts before our eyes and minds? Would Emmanuel use presence ("being with," or empathy) to convey the message of the heart as much as the interpretation of Scripture or use of familiar signs? Is this story typical of Emmanuel? Now, put yourself in the scene and let it unfold as the Holy Spirit directs.

VII. The Prodigal Son (Lk 15:11–32)

The parable of the prodigal son is Jesus' consummate revelation of the identity of God the Father. While revealing the nature of forgiveness and love, it shows the Father to be the fullest expression of that love. Some of Jesus' detractors were accusing Him of unjustifiably seeking fellowship with sinners. Jesus justifies His actions by noting that His conduct is completely commensurate with His Father's (*Abba*), Who is absolutely concerned for sinners and is capable of justifying even those who have abandoned and shamed their families, countrymen, the law, the covenant, and even God. The love of the father in this parable (who represents God the Father) is as close to an image of Unconditional Love as first-century Jewish images can portray. A retelling of the story as a first-century Semitic audience might have understood it will be helpful in appreciating one of Jesus' most powerful revelations of the love of God.

Once upon a time there was a father who had two sons. The youngest of the two said to his father, "[G]ive me the share of property that falls to me." This might be roughly translated as, "Father, you are as good as dead to me. The only worth you have is the inheritance money you can give me. Why don't you give it to me now and I will leave." The culture of the time would have viewed the son's actions to be appalling. The son has not only abandoned his father (breaking with filial duty), but also *shamed* the father (and the rest of the family) for everyone to see. A variety of reactions would have been appropriate for the father: mourning, anger, or rejection (disowning the son). But instead, the reaction of the father is virtually unpredictable; for instead of arguing with or disowning the boy, he simply divides the property and gives the boy his share. This is a very striking view of God in first-century Semitic culture, but it seems to betoken the unconditional Love of the Father (which continues to be revealed throughout the parable).

The boy then proceeds to a foreign land, the land of the Gentiles, where he spends his father's hard-earned wealth. This action would probably have been viewed by Jesus' audience as a rejection of his election (belonging to the chosen people), because he prefers to live with the foreign group rather than his own. In doing this, the boy has probably brought additional shame upon his father's household. But Jesus continues to reveal the son's deficits (which, in the eyes of His audience, would seem to be depravity).

Upon arriving in the foreign land, the boy proceeds to spend his father's fortune on dissolute living (violating the Torah—the Jewish law). This constitutes a rejection not only of the law of God, but also of God Himself, which brings additional shame to his family. Though the boy has now rejected and shamed family, country, election, law, and God, Jesus continues to recount the son's deficits.

He notes that the land experiences a famine, and the boy finds himself having to live with the pigs (which, according to the culture, are very unclean animals). In addition to showing the dire straits that the boy is in, Jesus is also indicating that the boy is in a state of profound ritual impurity. Jesus' audience would have thought "touching a pig" to be a serious matter. "Living with the pigs" and eating their food—bringing impurity to the inside as well as the outside—would be absolutely unthinkable. The portrayal of the boy is now complete. He has not only shamed and sinned against his family, election, people, law, and God; he has also managed to make himself thoroughly ritually impure.

Jesus abruptly changes the story by revealing that the boy comes to his senses (out of sheer desperation). He says to himself, "How many of my father's hired servants have bread enough and to spare, but I perish here with hunger! I will arise and go to my father, and I will say to him, 'Father, I have sinned against heaven and before you; I am no longer worthy to be called your son; treat me as one of your hired servants.'" The son takes his prepared speech and begins the long journey back home. But Jesus' listeners think they know what will happen when he gets near the territory of his father.

If his father's servants spot him before he steps foot on the property, he is likely to be held at the frontier until the father can deal with him as his actions deserve (according to justice in the law). This might result in a proclamation of disownership, a simple rejection, a banishment, or, in an unusual case, the father could take the son up on his offer to be a hired hand within the family domain (which would not only have reduced him to the means and status of a servant, but humiliated him). But this is not what happens.

Jesus surprises His audience by giving a "disappointing" ending (by the culture's standard of justice). Instead of the boy getting his "just desserts," the father is looking for him and is moved to show him mercy. Jesus says, "While he was yet at a distance, his father saw him" (v. 20). This conjures up the Rubens painting of the father standing at the pinnacle of his home with his hand cupped over his forehead, *looking* for his *beloved* son. When the father sees the son coming, he ignores the protocol of the day and runs out to meet the son on the son's turf. When he reaches him, he throws his arms around him and kisses him. The boy's sinfulness and ritual impurity (which would have made him untouchable) seem to be insignificant in comparison to the father's love, affection, and joy upon his son's return. Even though the son has nearly extinguished his own goodness and belovedness, his father recognizes in the son's sheer desperation a way to bestow his mercy and love.

At this juncture, Jesus becomes even more radical in His portrayal of the father's *unconditional* Love. When the son makes his offer to become a hired hand, the father is completely beyond it. He does not lecture his son about the injury and disgrace he has brought to his family; indeed, he does not even have a retributive word, not even a retributive mood! He simply throws his arms around his son and kisses him.

Needless to say, Jesus' audience must have been amazed. Instead of seeking just retribution, the father can't seem to give up the goodness and belovedness of his wayward son. No matter what the son has done extrinsically to almost kill this belovedness within himself, the father seems to see the glimmer of it not merely in the boy he loves, but also in the boy's attempt at contrition: "Father, I have sinned against heaven and before you; I am no longer worthy to be called your son, treat me as one of your hired servants. . . ." Though the father knows the heart of his son, the expression of contrition (which was somewhat imperfect in his attempt to bargain on the basis of a status reduction from son to servant) is radically accepted by the father. The son's need for the father and for his forgiveness is more than enough for the father.

At this point, the reader might want to look at Rembrandt's painting of the prodigal son's return. Notice the look of pure reveling in the father's eyes, as he hugs the son kneeling before him. Notice, too, the hands of the father—one very strong and masculine, the other considerably smaller, softer, and more feminine (see Nouwen, 1995). Notice the complete absence of anger in the scene, the sense of almost pastoral peace that exists through the embrace. In my view, Rembrandt has captured Jesus' consummate revelation of God the Father almost perfectly.

The father then turns to one of the servants to take care of the boy's temporal needs: "Bring quickly the best robe, and put it on him, and put a ring on his hand, and shoes on his feet." If we assume that first-century Jewish culture would have considered the ring to either have some familial significance or be a family treasure, then the father's gesture goes beyond lavishing luxury upon his son, to offering a family commitment to his son (much like our contemporary custom of a wedding ring). The father, then, is not merely restoring the boy back to health, or even to the *status* of a son, but also to full loving membership within the family. The reconciliation is unconditional and complete. The only thing that remains is to celebrate it. The father orders that the fatted calf be killed and the celebration begin.

Through these images, Jesus reveals at once the *unconditional* Love of the Father, His own unconditional Love in relation to the Father's, the need for unconditional forgiveness to prevent the needless waste of an intrinsically precious life (even though that life was *extrinsically* anything but precious), and the validity of His ministry to reach out in mercy to even the greatest sinners.

Jesus still has part two of the story left to tell. While the first part of the story is transpiring, the older son is still working diligently in the fields for the father and family. His loyalties and virtues seem unquestionable according to the standards of the time. He hears the music, merriment, and dancing and calls one of the servants over to ask about it. The servant informs him that his brother has returned, and that his father has not only met with him, but accepted him back into the family and is now having a celebration for him, killing the fatted calf. Given the shame that his younger brother has brought on the family, and the disloyalty he has shown to his people, election, the law, and his God, the older son is understandably dismayed, for justice demands some penalty, and, in the case of his brother, probably an extreme penalty. His father's unqualified acceptance of him back into the family is not only unintelligible; it cuts him to the core. He has been loyal; he has worked hard; he deserves better than this, and there are interpretations of the law that would allow his father to justifiably exact a penalty or retribution. He then refuses to come into the house.

When his father hears of this, he comes out to meet his son (again disregarding normal protocol) and begins to plead with him. A father's pleading in any culture, particularly this one, is unbecoming, yet he is willing to do it in order to bring his older son back to the house. It might be thought that this is where the analogy to God the Father breaks down. After all, would God plead with us? Would He take the lower place, even humiliate

Himself, to bring us, as it were, back into His house when we have refused to enter? Jesus knows well that both He and the Father would do far more than endure humiliation for our sake. Jesus would endure suffering and death (and His Father would endure the death of His Beloved). Here, only the logic of unconditional Love can make sense of the Father's actions.

The father begins his pleading with an acknowledgment of the older son's goodness, followed by an unconditional promise: "Son, you are always with me, and all that is mine is yours." Then, he goes on to explain his actions—the actions that do not make sense in the logic of strict justice, but do make sense in the logic of love, because they allow a nearly extinguished life to be resurrected, a state of misery to be rectified, a life lesson to be learned, and, above all, a family to be reconstituted (which was hurt by the absence of the younger son and was in need of his irreplaceable presence). The father sees the anguish of the son that needs to be redressed, and the complete waste entailed by the demise of his younger son, and so he says, "For this your brother was dead, and is alive; he was lost, and is found." This is the logic of unconditional Love, the heart of God the Father, and the essence of His Son, Who manifested the Father's heart through His words and on the Cross. Now, put yourself in the scene and let it unfold as the Holy Spirit directs.

VIII. A Note on Contemplating the Mysteries of the Rosary

If the above contemplations have provided you with a deepened experience of the heart of Jesus, then you will also want to make recourse to one of the Church's most powerful approaches to daily contemplation, namely, the Rosary. As noted above, the Hail Mary prayer brings with it a deep sense of comfort, healing, and peace—a sense that "everything is going to be alright." It also brings a deep sense of belonging to the Holy Family, and along with it a sense of the communion of saints, the Mystical Body, the Church, and our eternal Home. All of this is linked through Mary to the historical Jesus. It is like tapping into the events of Jesus' life through the memory and feelings of His Mother. What better prayer could there be to ground contemplation on the mysteries of Jesus' life?

The Rosary has played a very special part in the development of my own contemplative life. Though my daily prayer is oriented around the Holy Eucharist and the breviary, I frequently feel invited to pray the Rosary and meditate on its mysteries when little windows of opportunity present themselves. I do not feel obligated to pray the whole Rosary, but only as many decades as meaningful contemplation and time permit. It is much better to pray the Rosary slowly (so that one can hear the intercessory prayer to Mary echoing in one's mind as one contemplates the heart of Jesus in one or two mysteries) than to rapidly move through the whole Rosary in order to finish it. I have frequently felt God's deep consolation in these little windows of opportunity, which have made me aware of the presence of the Father, Jesus, and/or the Holy Spirit (through the intercession of Mary). These consolations have helped me to keep my mind and heart focused on the Beatitudes and have helped me follow the guidance of the Holy Spirit throughout the day. Sometimes they have actually called me back from the doldrums, and from errant thoughts and courses of action. Sometimes I simply feel like praying a few decades after my breviary because the invitation seems so delightful, beautiful, and "completing." Sometimes the Rosary is the only way of calming my racing thoughts before I go to sleep. Indeed, its power to calm, center, and induce contemplation in the most spontaneous windows of the busiest days cannot be overestimated.

There are Scripture passages corresponding to eighteen of the twenty mysteries of the Rosary. The two Marian glorious mysteries may be found in subsequent Church doctrines (references are given below). If you prefer to make these contemplations on the basis of Scripture alone, you will want to make recourse to the following passages:

The Joyful Mysteries

6. The Annunciation (Lk 1:26–38)
7. The Visitation to Elizabeth (Lk 1:39–56)
8. The Nativity of Jesus (Lk 2:7–19; Mt 2:1–11)
9. The Presentation (Lk 2:22–40)
10. The Finding of the Child Jesus in the Temple (Lk 2:41–52)

The Luminous Mysteries (optional)

1. The Baptism of Jesus (Mt 3:13–17; Mk 1:10; Lk 3:21–22; and partial par. in Jn 1:29–34)
2. The Wedding Feast at Cana (Jn 2:1–11)
3. The Proclamation of the Kingdom (Mt 4:17 and parallels, Mt 5:1–7:29; Lk 6:20–49)

4. The Transfiguration of Jesus (Mk 9:2–8; Mt 17:1–8; Lk 9:28–36)
5. The Institution of the Holy Eucharist (Mk 14:22–25; Lk 22:17–19; Mt 26:26–29; 1 Cor 11:23–29)

The Sorrowful Mysteries

1. The Agony in the Garden (Mk 14:32–52; Mt 26:36–56; Lk 22:39–46; Jn 18:1–12)
2. The Scourging at the Pillar (Mk 15:15; Mt 27:26; Jn 19:1)
3. The Crowning with Thorns (Mk 15:17–20; Mt 27:27–31; Jn 19:2–3)
4. The Way of the Cross (Mk 15:20–23; Mt 27:31–34; Lk 23:26–32; Jn 19:16–17)
5. The Crucifixion (Mk 15:24–37; Mt 27:35–50; Lk 23:33–46; Jn 19:18–34)

The Glorious Mysteries

1. The Resurrection
   The list of the witnesses (1 Cor 15)
   The appearance to the women (Mt 28:8–10)
   The appearance to the Eleven (Mt 28:16–20)
   Appearance to the disciples on the road to Emmaus (Lk 24:13–32)
   Appearance to the Eleven in the closed room (Lk 24:36–52)
   Appearance to Mary Magdalene (Jn 20:14–18)
   Jesus appears to the Ten without Thomas in the closed room (Jn 20:19–23)

> *Jesus appears to the Eleven with Thomas in the closed room* (Jn 20:26–29)
>
> *Jesus appears to the disciples on the Sea of Tiberias* (Jn 21:1–25)

2. The Ascension (Lk 24:50–52; Acts 1:9–11)
3. The Descent of the Holy Spirit (Acts 2:1–42)
4. The Assumption of the Blessed Virgin Mary. The Assumption of Mary is an ancient tradition in the Church and arose out of the conviction that Mary, as Mother of the risen Jesus, would experience risen life in a way commensurate with her Son. According to the Second Vatican Council:

> Finally, preserved free from all guilt of original sin, the Immaculate Virgin was taken up body and soul into heavenly glory upon the completion of her earthly sojourn. She was exalted by the Lord as Queen of all, in order that she might be the more thoroughly conformed to her Son, the Lord of lords (cf. Apoc. 19:16) and the conqueror of sin and death. (*Lumen Gentium*, no. 59)

5. The Coronation (Queenship) of Mary. As implied in the above quotation from the Second Vatican Council, Mary's assumption proceeded naturally to her exaltation with her Son. This gave her a special role in the continuing economy of salvation.

There are many excellent volumes that can give you a deeper insight into the above Scripture texts of the Rosary. Two excellent ones are *The Magnificat Rosary Companion* and *Rosary: The Chain of Hope—Meditations on the Mysteries of the Rosary with 20 Renaissance Paintings*, by Benedict Groeschel.

There is a lifetime of contemplative opportunity contained in the Rosary's meditations as well as those contained in the Scriptures. There is also significant contemplative material in the breviary and in daily prayer publications such as the *Magnificat* and *The Word Among Us* (see chapter 8, section I).

Chapter Eight

Fifth Pillar: The Contemplative Life (*Continued*)— Contemplation in Everyday Life

Introduction

The contemplative life connects God's heart to one's own through praise, then gratitude, and then the freedom to love (the freedom of the Beatitudes). In everyday life, these dynamics build on themselves in an ever-widening spiral. Each of these elements will be discussed in turn.

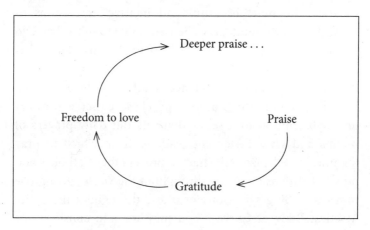

I. Praise

Lest anyone think that God wants us to praise Him to meet "His ego needs," it should be noted that giving praise to God brings *us* into contact with the heart of God, and, as a consequence, incites delight within us, puts *our* universe in order, brings *us* peace, purifies *our* desire, helps *us* to see the places where we need forgiveness and light, helps *us* to recognize what we have to be grateful for, allows the Beatitudes to flow freely from us, transforms *us* in the heart of Christ, and makes *us* free to act in accordance with the love of God. God desires our praise because it encourages our freedom to love, our joy and peace, and our eternal destiny. In view of its incredible importance, it is essential for everyone to devote at least ten to fifteen minutes per day to this life-enhancing, all-pervading, and beautiful activity.

Prayers of praise have been commonplace in the Judeo-Christian tradition for over three thousand years. The Psalms (though sometimes superseded in their cosmology, aggression toward enemies, and views of vengeance) are some of the most beautiful and incisive expressions of God's love and grandeur. When combined with other Old Testament canticles, New Testament hymns, and New Testament readings, they provide a context for reveling in the majesty, beauty, providence, truth, and love of God. I would recommend that you purchase either a breviary or a subscription to a series that sets out daily prayers of psalms and New Testament readings from which to pray the prayer of the Church (that is, prayers that Catholics and other Christians are using throughout the world, giving rise to a resounding symphony of praise throughout the entire Mystical Body of Christ). You may want to consider one of the following two series *or* one of the two editions of the breviary.

1. The *Word Among Us* is a monthly series of psalms and Mass readings for the day in an easy-to-follow format.

2. The *Magnificat* contains the psalms and Mass readings for the day, as well as a variety of meditations and additional prayers.

3. *Christian Prayer* (which is a one-volume edition of the Catholic breviary—the Divine Office) contains morning prayer, evening prayer, daytime prayer (selections), and night prayer. It does not include the Office of Readings.

4. *Shorter Christian Prayer.* This is a shorter version of the Divine Office with only morning and evening prayer.

I would recommend either *The Word Among Us* or *Magnificat* for those who are beginning the contemplative life. The editors have designed these volumes for active lay people with various levels of preparation.

All of the above resources are designed to promote routine. Newcomers may want to begin with morning prayer by setting aside ten to fifteen minutes each morning. This might be done by waking up earlier, or, if you go to daily Mass, prior to or after Mass. If a routine begins to develop, then you might want to proceed to evening prayer and cultivate another routine.

It is far more important to develop a routine around prayers that truly inspire you than to "do it all." Thus, if you have only ten minutes in the morning and you are doing the breviary, you may want to do the three psalms, the reading, the responsory, and the Our Father. These prayers tend to be the most inspiring for general audiences. The key is to stick to this routine every day, and to make the most of it. How does one make the most of it? You might bear in mind the following thoughts.

First, do not get overly anxious about outdated theologies or cosmologies in the Psalms. When you see phrases that seem to be incompatible with the Beatitudes, simply glance over them as if they are the product of an ancient quasi-warrior culture (which they are). Second, concentrate on the beautiful phrases—the ones that express profound wonder, delight, and love in the glory and grandeur of God, or in the glorious works of His hands, or in His work and guidance in Jerusalem, or in the beauty of His law, etc. Revel in the truth, goodness, and beauty of phrases such as: "Like the deer that yearns for running streams, so my heart is yearning for You, my God," or, "How lovely is Your dwelling place, Lord, God of hosts," or, "How wonderful are Your works, O Lord, through all the earth," or, "Mighty and wonderful are Your works, Lord, God Almighty; righteous and true are Your ways, O King of the universe." Third, pray the psalm slowly enough so that the images, metaphors, emotions, intuitions, trust, and hope can begin to touch you.

The Psalms are remarkable in the range of emotions they portray, the petitions they make to God, the deep trust they have in His providence, and, above all, the delight and reverie they display for God's power, love, majesty, truth, goodness, care, holiness, and trustworthiness. They state these truths of the heart with both innocence and starkness (as if out of the mouths of babes and spiritually mature people, simultaneously). They exemplify sheer pleasure and delight in recounting the works and deeds of God, and, most of all, in the goodness of God Himself. If we think about, probe, and feel the recurrent awe-filled and affectionate themes, we cannot help but share the psalmists' delight.

As Christians, we can go beyond the psalmists' delight. We can think of and delight in the fuller meaning of God's redemption (in Jesus Christ), the new Jerusalem as well as the old, the lives of the saints as well as the prophets, and the works of the Lord in the Church (through the Holy Spirit) as well as in ancient Israel. We can apply the insights of the psalmists and the readings to the problems of today.

Furthermore, the above resources integrate New Testament canticles and readings into the Psalms. The New Testament canticles focus on Jesus Christ—His mission, messiahship, divinity, humility, love, and glory. The New Testament readings from Paul, John, James, and Peter focus on lessons for life, movement toward the Beatitudes, and gratitude for everything around us. They make a remarkably integrated weave of praise amidst instruction, and instruction amidst praise. They stimulate the desire for God, the theological imagination, the heart of love, and the appreciation of divine mystery filled, as it is, with awe.

This mixture of psalms and New Testament canticles and readings has a peculiar power. As noted in chapter 3, it allows God to come back into the center of our universe (after we have tried to take His place) and allows us to graciously resume our proper place as coequals with others in the surrounding area. This "proper perspective" enables us to reenkindle our Level 4 desire to live for God, His kingdom, and His will as if it were the only real purpose of our lives (which it is). It then allows the other three levels of desire to find their proper place in relation to the fourth. At this juncture, surrender becomes possible; so also peace arising out of detachment from desires of lesser importance; so also the ability to place ourselves (in complete trust) in the providential care of God. This is freedom—true freedom—the freedom to let go of everything that is not of God, which is less than "unconditional Truth, Love, Goodness, Beauty, and Being."

This freedom opens the way to remarkably efficacious partnership with the Holy Spirit (in inspiration, guidance, peace during times of suffering, transformation, projects for the kingdom of God, creativity, discernment, and animated action—see chapter 4). It also unlocks our potential to love and live for the Beatitudes (chapter 3). It is remarkable to me how I can love humble-heartedness, gentle-heartedness, forgiveness, and mercy while I am delighting in the glory and mystery of God. It is even more remarkable how this love of the Beatitudes brings with it a peace and a desire to live for them in my life—while I am actually praying about how God is like Mount Zion, or His power like lightning, or His truth reaching to the skies. The simple recitation of psalms, canticles, and readings quickens and purifies our desire for God, our desire for His will, our love of the Beatitudes, and our desire to live the Beatitudes. It imparts peace and confidence, hope and trust. It even enables me to recall my need for forgiveness and the many blessings for which I am grateful. Above all, the Psalms set the tone of joy. As the responsory so often notes, "It is my joy, O God, to praise You with song."

It may be difficult to believe that so much depth can rise to the surface of our hearts, and so much grace, peace, and joy can be infused in us through so simple an enterprise, with such simple words, from people of such simple faith, so long ago. Yet that is what the recitation of morning and evening prayer does, for the Holy Spirit speaks to us with ineffable groanings, with a peace beyond all understanding, with an intimate knowledge of *Abba* (the loving Father), and with the knowledge of the mind and heart of God.

Why spend fifteen minutes on morning prayer, fifteen minutes on the contemplative life? The answer by now should be obvious. The gifts, graces, love, peace, joy, inspiration, insight, creativity, and animation of this enterprise transforms not only the *quality* of every *action* in which we are engaged, but also our very *hearts*, preparing us for the life and kingdom of love to come. The time spent in contemplation is the most important fifteen minutes of the day. Without it, our hearts can barely scratch the surface of their potential, and our actions are left bereft of their true depth and quality. Saint Ignatius was right—we need to be contemplatives in action.

II. From Gratitude to the Freedom to Love: The Examen Prayer

Gratitude is the second act of contemplation and the spiritual life (following upon praise). It is no accident that the Greek word "*eucharistia*" means "thanksgiving," for that is precisely what Jesus was doing when He initiated the precious sacrament of His unconditional Love. As a consequence, the whole of Christian spiritual tradition is premised on receiving the gifts and graces that God continually presents to us. But such reception depends on our recognizing these gifts. If we do not recognize as wondrous gifts the gifts of life, love, other people, family, good things, goodness itself, being rescued from danger, being "on the right road," the beauty of nature, beauty itself, education, creativity, the truth itself, and even the desire and capacity to give praise to God—gifts that so easily could have been absent, indeed, which so easily could have been otherwise—then we are probably destined to see life in terms of what we lack, what we do *not* have, or what we did *not* get, etc. Dissatisfaction with what we lack leads to resentment and self-pity, while gratitude recognizes the loving hand of God. The latter is the condition necessary for the spiritual life; the former undermines it.

This fundamental orientation toward gratitude pertains not only to the spiritual life, but to life and happiness itself. There is an old expression that runs as follows: "I never knew a grateful person who was unhappy, or an ungrateful person who was happy." This is a truism because a lack of gratitude generally reveals "taking things for granted," that is, assuming that things *should* be better than they are, or even that things *should* be perfect. When "things" fall short of this idealistic expectation, disappointment, frustration, self-pity, and resentment soon follow. If this becomes our general state of mind, we are likely to be unhappy.

Conversely, if we do not assume that things should be better than they are (or even perfect), but rather are surprised by how good things are (when they could be otherwise), then life is filled with pleasant surprises and wonder at the goodness that need not be. Instead of taking life for granted, we feel fortunate, special, and "taken care of" amidst natural forces that might have otherwise been indifferent to our well-being. Inasmuch as we don't live in a state of perfection, we must face challenges, but these challenges are not necessarily negative; they are opportunities to develop courage, self-discipline, compassion, self-sacrifice, wisdom, care, and love (virtues that must be freely chosen and are best recognized through challenge and even adversity). Thus, we can even be grateful for adversity and challenge, for these might be the vehicles for freely appropriating what truly makes life worth living, what truly constitutes the core of our fully developed selves. Grateful people, then, not only find life full of wonder and surprise, not only see themselves as taken care of, but also seize upon challenge to move toward virtue and love. Grateful people can be on a journey, can be led, and can find themselves being drawn into the fullness of life and love by the perfection they do not yet have, but long for with all their hearts. Grateful people are not only happy; they have a capacity for a spiritual journey culminating in the perfection of love. And that makes all the difference.

I do not mean to be insensitive here to people who are experiencing extreme tragedy. God does know how awful such experiences can be for us, and He knows how only time and grace can heal. It is far more important for people in these circumstances to rest in the peace of Christ than to feel any kind of conjured or artificial gratitude for what they cannot yet perceive to be positive. Nevertheless, in the course of graces' healing time, gratitude will once again become the road to serenity, happiness, and, yes, the love that is the objective of the spiritual life and even life itself.

Another clarification may prove helpful. One might think that grateful people are more likely to sit on their laurels because the motivation to change or improve is frequently caused by discontent, and grateful people seem to be quite content. But one must remember that there are at least two motives for change and improvement. The first might be discontent with the present, but the second (and by no means the inferior) is the desire to see the actualization of an improved condition because it will advance the cause of the community, the culture, the common good, the will of God, or the kingdom of God. Motivation to improve, then, need not arise out of being discontent; it can more frequently and powerfully arise out of the desire to see the actualization of an improved condition for humanity and the kingdom of God. Idealists generally leave deeper and more extensive legacies than malcontents. The former take their lead from Level 3 and Level 4 desires, while the latter take theirs from Level 1 and Level 2 desires. Inasmuch as Level 3 and Level 4 move beyond themselves, and Level 4 desires are oriented toward eternity, it should come as no surprise that their deeper and more pervasive effects will endure much longer (see the epilogue to this book).

There is yet another important clarification to be made. We may be under the mistaken impression that the centrality of gratitude in the spiritual life arises out of God's *need* (or even greed) for our gratitude. God no doubt delights in our gratitude, but not because He needs it for ego-fulfillment! God delights in our openness to being led, in our acceptance of challenge, and in our awareness of the goodness of the life we have been given, filled as it is with partial positivity, openness to the free choice of virtue and love, and the prospect for unconditional Love. God delights in us delighting in the goodness of the condition into which we have been born. Yes, it is fraught with challenges (and even deep suffering), but in each of these challenges lies the opportunity for the free pursuit of love, which is our destiny and salvation. God delights in us recognizing and delighting in the wisdom-toward-love into which we have been born, for it is in this recognition that we will find true happiness, which, in turn, brings happiness to God. God does not delight in our prayer because it boosts His ego. He delights in us praying to Him because it brings *us* peace, freedom-toward-love, transformation, and ultimate happiness. God is happy when we are on the road to true happiness.

Saint Ignatius well recognized the centrality of gratitude in the pursuit of contemplation and the love of God, and so he made it the essence of his famous "Contemplation on Divine Love" (the final contemplation in the Spiritual Exercises). A few of his preludes in this famous contemplation will make this point clear:

> This is to ask for what I desire. Here it will be to ask for an intimate knowledge of the many blessings received, that filled with gratitude for all, I may in all things love and serve the Divine Majesty.
>
> First Point. This is to recall to mind the blessings of creation and redemption, and the special favors I have received.
>
> I will ponder with great affection how much God our Lord has done for me, and how much He has given me of what He possesses, and finally, how much, as far as He can, the same Lord desires to give *Himself* to me according to His divine decrees. (Saint Ignatius of Loyola 1951, pp. 101–2)

Saint Ignatius expects that most people will be filled with gratitude, and through this gratitude will feel great love for the Lord, Who has loved us. He believes that this love, in turn, will purify our Level 4 desire (our hearts), which will motivate us to make ourselves instruments of the Lord's optimal love, goodness, justice, and salvation in the world. So he presents his famous prayer (the *Suscipe*) given earlier:

> Take, Lord, receive all my liberty,
>
> my memory, my understanding, and my entire will, all that I have
>   and possess.
>
> Thou hast given all to me.
>
> To Thee, O Lord, I return it. All is Thine, dispose of it wholly
>   according to Thy will.
>
> Give me Thy love and Thy grace, for this is sufficient for me. (p. 102)

We now need to reflect on how to savor this spiritual gratitude, which engenders freedom to love.

Saint Ignatius gave his followers a very powerful tool for savoring gratitude called the Examen. It has two parts: (1) a recognition of the many blessings we have received (which engenders gratitude), and (2) a reflection on how we might move with Christ more deeply into the Beatitudes (manifesting His love).

1.   *First Part of the Examen.* Saint Ignatius hoped that we would be able to recall, at least once per day (in imitation of the "Contemplation on Divine Love"), some of the blessings that God has given us. I find it particularly helpful to make this recollection after giving praise to God (perhaps by praying the psalms in my breviary), because, as noted above, these prayers place God squarely in the center of the universe, while placing me as one co-equal part of the surrounding environment. As I move from one psalm to the next, I find that this "proper perspective" engenders the need for forgiveness and also deep gratitude for various blessings that seem to pop into my head. At the end of my prayers, I take a few moments to reflect on these times of needed

forgiveness and the blessings I have received. Gratitude and love naturally follow, as Saint Ignatius expected.

For whatever reason, I do not have to make a formal meditation on the blessings I have received during the day, week, or even during my lifetime. They seem to pop up very naturally in my prayer of praise. However, I have been told by others that they receive more fruit when they go through a list of general items representing areas in which they may have been blessed, such as in their families, church lives, friendships, workplaces, community lives, service lives, intellectual lives, moral lives, and even recreational lives. One need not use such a list, but as Saint Ignatius said, use these tools insofar as they are helpful; avoid them insofar as they are not.

During my Examen (after giving praise to God in the psalms and canticles), I try to picture God presenting me with the blessings I have recalled from the previous day or week, for this expresses the reality of what has actually occurred. As I picture God giving me these blessings (even the ones that may be superficially unpleasant, but fundamentally very important), I feel great affection for Him. I then take a moment to *converse* with Him about things of import. Sometimes this concerns events coming up during the day; sometimes it concerns areas in which I want to improve (such as asking for the grace to be more patient, or to look for the good news in other people, or to be more humble during the day). Sometimes it concerns the Beatitudes themselves— thinking about the wisdom or beauty of them, or, more often, thinking about the wisdom, beauty, and love of the One who proposed them. In any event, I feel quite free to discuss all these matters (including my love for the One with whom I'm doing the discussing) as I go along. This leads to the next part of my Examen.

2. *Second Part of the Examen.* This part consists in a prayer about the Beatitudes. My intention here is not to go over the content of chapter 3 in an intellectual reflection, but rather to ask the Lord for help in imitating *Him* in the pursuit of the Beatitudes. Hence, I offer a very simple prayer and ask the Holy Spirit to awaken my heart so that I might understand the beauty of this teaching more deeply and live it more authentically. My prayer goes as follows:

> Lord, Jesus, help me to be humble-hearted with You, Who are humble of heart.
>
> Help me to be gentle-hearted with You, Who are gentle of heart.
>
> Help me to be holy with You, the source of holiness.
>
> Help me to be forgiving and merciful with You, Who are forgiving and merciful.
>
> Help me to be pure of heart with You, Who are pure of heart.
>
> Help me to be a peacemaker with You, the consummate peacemaker.

As I move through this little prayer, the Holy Spirit reveals not only that I am a companion of Jesus on the journey, but also that He helps me, heals me, and forgives me in His humility, gentleness, and purity of heart. The Holy Spirit awakens ways in which I can deepen these Beatitudes in my heart and also allows me to carry this prayer into the actions of my day. Though I live the Beatitudes very imperfectly, the prayer provides a vehicle through which my imperfection can sometimes be overcome by grace. Over the course of time, these little graces, these little "overcomings of imperfection by grace," build on themselves, and real transitions in the heart and love of Christ begin to take place. And that makes all the difference.

I am fully cognizant that I cannot give this grace to myself, for whenever I have tried to be humble-hearted on my own, I have found myself more proud; whenever I have tried to compel myself to gentle-heartedness, I have found myself more harsh; whenever I have tried to compel myself to forgiveness, I play the tapes of my being offended with greater vigor; and whenever I try to compel myself to mercy, I find myself forgetting the marginalized. The reader may have more natural virtue than I do, but in the absence of natural virtue, I am able to recognize, with great acuity, how very special the purity of Level 4 desire, humble-heartedness, gentle-heartedness, forgiveness, mercy, and peacemaking really are. I feel truly graced when the Beatitudes pop out of me, when I truly love them, and when I feel alienated when I do not accommodate them. It is this final blessing that makes my heart rejoice in the Lord of love most of all. I almost instinctively say the prayer of Jesus, "I thank you, Father, Lord of heaven and earth, that you have hidden these things from the wise and understanding and revealed them to infants, yes, Father, for such was your gracious will" (Mt 11:25–26). I am the infant, the recipient of the revelation, and, once again, I am moved in gratitude to love Him.

I then conclude my prayer in the way that Saint Ignatius concludes the *Spiritual Exercises*—that is, with the prayer that is at once an expanded rendition of "Thy will be done," an offering of myself, and my hope for being the instrument of His optimally loving, good, just, and salvific will (the *Suscipe*: "Take, Lord, receive all my liberty. . . .").

After saying this prayer, I sometimes feel like it's time to go. Sometimes, however, it seems appropriate to just hang around God "on absorb" (rather like Mary at the feet of Jesus, while Martha is expressing frustration). Sometimes this "hanging around" gives rise to spiritual insight or consolation; sometimes it is just silence (which may well be God waiting for me to think or do something).

As my prayer concludes, I notice a sense of restored equanimity, a balance, a confidence about living in His presence, an openness to the Beatitudes, and a purity of the desire for Him, His kingdom, and His will.

Upon completion of my contemplation, I depend on the loving power of the Eucharist and the inspiration of the Holy Spirit to carry my gratitude and love more deeply into my heart and more decisively into the world of action. The time spent in contemplation not only empowers and deepens my spontaneous prayers; it also works its way into my heart, and ever, ever so gently and gradually, transforms me so that I am drawn to the true reality of Jesus, who has called me into His very life of love with the Father. I leave the rest to the Holy Spirit, Who will find ways to effect a nexus between contemplation and action.

Epilogue

The Stages on Life's Way:
Four Levels of Desire and Happiness

The four levels of desire (or happiness) have been mentioned several times throughout this book—principally, in chapter 1 (section IV), and chapter 3 (section I). This epilogue is provided for those readers who are interested in a more systematic explanation of these four levels and the ways in which grace and prayer interact through them.

In two of my other works (*Healing the Culture* and *The Spirit of Leadership*—see References), I describe these four levels of happiness in detail. Normally, one of these desires becomes dominant, and the others become either recessive or ignored. The dominant desire becomes our identity, while recessive ones serve the dominant one. Ignored desires generally frustrate or debilitate us. Even though all four desires are functional, the dominant desire (or identity) tends to control the way we view happiness and success, our goals in life, the way we conduct relationships and view love, our principles and ethics, the ideals we seek, and the way we judge our self-worth, our progress in life, and our very selves. Needless to say, the kind of desire we choose or allow to

Four Levels of Desire/Happiness

	Ultimate or Unconditional Purpose
4	**Objective:** Seek and live in ultimate Truth, Love, Goodness, Justice, Beauty, and Being (Platonic transcendentals).
	Characteristics: Seeking the unconditional, unrestricted, perfect, eternal in above trancendentals. Can come from pursuit of transcendentals or faith/God/religion. Optimal pervasiveness, endurance, and depth.
	Contributive (Ego-out)
3	**Objective:** Optimize positive difference in the world. (The world is better off for my having lived.) Comes from "doing for" and "being with."
	Characteristics: More pervasive (positive effects beyond self), enduring (lasts longer), and deep (using highest creative and psychological powers). Can come from generosity, magnanimity, altruism, love.
	Comparative (Ego-in)
2	**Objective:** Shift locus of control to self (ego) and gain comparative advantage (in status, esteem, power, control, winning, and success.)
	Characteristics: Intense ego-gratification (sense of progress, superiority, and esteemability). If dominant, then fear of failure, ego-sensitivity, ego-blame/rage, self-pity, inferiority, suspicion, resentment.
	Physical/External Stimulus
1	**Objective:** The pleasure or material object itself (nothing beyond this).
	Characteristics: Immediate gratification, surface apparent, and intensity of stimulus. No desire for common, intrinsic, or ultimate good.

become dominant is one of the most important decisions in our lives. Therefore, a more systematic explanation of these desires might be helpful to better understand the fourth level (the spiritual life).

Recall from chapter 1 (section IV) that Level 1 (*laetus*) is the desire for externally stimulated or physical pleasures and possessions (e.g., a bowl of linguini or a new Mercedes e-Class with leather upholstery).

Level 2 (*felix*) is an ego-gratification arising out of the displacement of the outer world toward my inner world (my *ego*—"I"). Such ego-gratifications might take the form of increases in status, admiration, achievement, power, control, winning, etc., and generally entail a comparative advantage, which can lead to fixation and extremely negative emotive conditions (see below).

The third level of happiness (*beatus*) moves in the opposite direction of Level 2. Instead of displacing the outer world toward my inner world (Level 2), it invests my inner world in the outer world, that is, it tries to make an optimal positive difference to the world (e.g., to family, friends, organization, community, church, culture, and kingdom of God) with my time, talents, energy, indeed, my life. It can occur through both action and "being with," and occurs most powerfully through *agape* (love without expectation of return—love for the sake of the beloved alone).

Level 4 (*sublimis*) is the desire for the ultimate, uncon-ditional, or perfect in Truth, Love, Goodness, Beauty, and Being. Faith identifies perfect and unconditional Truth, Love, Goodness, Beauty, and Being with God; and so Level 4, for people of faith, is the desire for God. Its fullest expression has been elucidated throughout this book.

The above four levels of desire (or happiness) may be summarized in this diagram:

As one moves *up* the four levels of desire, one attains more pervasive, enduring, and deep purpose in life. For example, Level 3 or 4 purpose has a much greater effect in the world (more *pervasive*) than a Level 1 or 2 purpose (which is restricted to *self*-benefit). Similarly, Level 3 and 4 purpose *endures* much longer than Level 1 or 2 purpose. Level 4 purpose even endures unto eternity. Finally, Level 3 or 4 purpose is *deeper* (utilizes our higher powers of creativity, intellection, moral reasoning, love, and spiritual awareness) than Level 1 or 2 purpose. If efficacy in life is determined by the pervasiveness, endurance, and depth of one's actions, then the higher one moves up the levels of desire, the greater the effectiveness of one's life.

The only "down side" to this ascendancy of effectiveness and purpose in life is that one has to delay gratification, look beneath and beyond the surface of life, and give up some degree of intensity. It is clear that Level 1 is immediately gratifying, surface apparent, and intense, while Level 4 frequently requires nuance, education, subtlety, delay in gratification, and detachment from intensity. Thus, the spiritual life is marked by a trade-off—in order to attain to universal and eternal effects arising out of our self-transcendent powers of Truth, Love, Goodness, Beauty, and Being, we frequently have to give up some degree of immediate gratification, intensity, and surface apparentness.

This "trade-off" marks one of the most difficult challenges of the spiritual life, for it is not easy to let go of what is so easily and intensely satisfying. Yet, it is worth it, for the move to Levels 3 and 4 fills us with higher purpose, more enduring (even eternal) effects, and awakens the highest, most sophisticated powers within us; and far more than this, Level 4 introduces us to a deep relationship with the unconditionally loving God (which the preceding chapters show is our purification and joy). Thus, Level 4 simultaneously actualizes our humanity and spiritual life. Saint Augustine phrased it well when he prayed to God, "For Thou hast made us for Thyself, and our hearts are restless until they rest in Thee."

As noted above, each level of desire can become dominant, and when it does, it becomes our purpose in life and our identity. As shown throughout the book, human beings can only be *ultimately* satisfied by a Level 4 identity, because our desire for the unconditional and perfect in Truth, Love, Goodness, Beauty, and Being can never be satiated by what is conditioned or imperfect. Inasmuch as God is the one and only unconditional and perfect Truth-Love-Goodness-Beauty-Being, then Saint Augustine was correct in his prayer.

Most of us do not come to this conclusion through an intuitive grasp of the truth of Saint Augustine's prayer. We normally do it through the school of hard knocks (much like Saint Augustine himself). We obsess upon the material/physical world (Level 1) and the ego/comparative world (Level 2) because they are so immediately gratifying, intense, and surface-apparent. It is hard to loosen our grip on them, even in order to pursue what is more pervasive, enduring, and deep; even to pursue what is eternal, perfect, and unconditional; even to pursue the ultimate fulfillment of our being. Thus, most of us move through a series of trials and tribulations that manifest the pain of overinvesting in what is beneath our ultimate dignity and nature. The most popular overinvestment in our culture is the one directed at Level 2, and so I will illustrate it here. I have written extensively about other overinvestments in both *Healing the Culture* and *The Spirit of Leadership* (see References).

Level 2 (ego-gratification) is almost always linked to comparisons. In order to shift the locus of control from the outer world to the inner world, I must constantly ask myself, "Who is achieving more? Who is achieving less? Who is making more progress? Who is making less? Who is winning? Who is losing? Who has got more status? Who has got less status? Who is more popular? Who is less popular? Who has got more control? Who has got less control? Who is more admired? Who is less admired?" Notice that these questions are not linked to a pursuit of the truth or to a contributive mentality, or even to an ultimate meaning. One is using these comparative questions to obtain identity. Thus, one is literally living for a Level 2 answer to these questions and is therefore treating these comparative characteristics as *ends in themselves*. Hence, one is not achieving in order to contribute to family, colleagues, or the culture; one is achieving as an end in itself, as if achievement gave life meaning. Similarly, one is not seeking status in order to have the credibility to do good for others or even the kingdom of God. One is simply seeking status as an end in itself. The same holds for winning, power, control, and so forth.

Notice further that Level 2 is not bad. Indeed, quite the opposite. The desire for achievement leads to progress in civilization. The desire for respect leads to credibility, confidence, and self-respect. The desire to win leads to competitiveness and the seeking of excellence. Even the desire for power can be used for good purposes. So what's the problem? The problem is not Level 2, but living for Level 2 *as an end in itself.* When one does this, then achievement leads to compulsive "getting ahead," instead of "a good beyond the achievement." Seeking respect leads to pandering after admiration. Power sought as an end in itself corrupts—and absolute power sought in itself corrupts absolutely.

A variety of consequences follows from this narrow purpose in life: one may feel emptiness arising out of "underliving life." The desire to make a positive difference (or even an optimal positive difference) to family, friends, community, organization, colleagues, church, culture, and society (Level 3) goes unfulfilled. One begins to think that one's life doesn't really make any difference to the world or to history: "The world is not better off for my having lived." To make matters worse, one's desire for the ultimate (in Truth, Love, Goodness, Beauty, and Being—indeed, God) is also unfulfilled. Though one longs for the ultimate with all one's heart, one's obsession with Level 2 precludes the pursuit of Level 4. Again, one's spirit reacts with a profound sense of emptiness, a sense of underliving life, a more and more poignant awareness that "I am wasting the little precious time I have in this world."

Furthermore, a large array of negative emotions begins to accompany this emptiness. Most of these emotions arise out of a fixation on comparative advantage. Since a dominant Level 2 identity treats status, admiration, power, control, winning, etc., as ends in themselves, it is compelled to seek comparative advantage as its fulfillment. This fixation requires not only that I progress more and more (in status, power, winning, and so forth), but also that I have *more* of it than Joe, Sue, Frank, and Mary. When I do not have more, when I am not better than others, I profoundly believe that my life is either stagnant or slipping away. I feel a profound diminishment in self-worth and success. And so I begin to feel jealousy, a malaise about life, inferiority, loneliness, frustration, and even a terrible sense of self-pity and resentment.

One might respond that these negative emotions do not befall the dominant Level 2 *winner*; for to the victor go the spoils. While it is true that winners do receive significant ego-gratification, it is worth noting that the above-mentioned emptiness still follows in its wake. Furthermore, such winners are obliged to increase in their Level 2 successes, because they cannot attain any sense of progress without doing so. If they do not continually increase in their successes, they experience the same kinds of malaise, inferiority, jealousy, frustration, and self-pity as nonwinners.

Moreover, these winners contract a peculiar disease, namely, the desire to be overtly admired. When perceived inferiors do not acknowledge the winner's superiority (and their own inferiority by comparison), the winner feels tremendous resentment. "You have not given me the accolades I deserve. And, furthermore, you are actually treating yourself as my equal—who do you think you are?" This peculiar disease has another aspect that Saint Augustine well recognized, namely, contempt. Dominant Level 2 winners can't help it. They really do feel that their lives are worth more than other people's lives, and so they either project contempt or (if they are more enlightened) they are patronizingly condescending ("That's a nice *little* project you did there"). In the end, such winners cannot afford to fail; if they do, those whom they have treated with contempt will ravage them.

Furthermore, a winner's self-image cannot tolerate being embarrassed in front of others. ("You pronounced the word 'spectroscopy' improperly three times. I cannot believe that a person of your caliber would make such a mistake." I go to my room, close the door, and play that excruciating tape over and over again in my mind until I want to do myself physical harm, for the physical pain would be so much better than ... "I can't believe I made that mistake in public. Aaarrgghh!"). Dominant Level 2 winners also feel the need to blame others for all their failures (because, in principle, they cannot fail).

In sum, winners better be perfect; but then again, they can't be altogether perfect. So winners must construct a huge facade and then protect it; but, then again, they cannot construct a facade impenetrable enough to keep observant inferiors at bay. So, dominant Level 2 winners better be prepared for contempt, resentment, blame, anger, debilitating ego sensitivities, and, above all, loneliness—for no one (except Mother Teresa, and maybe their own mothers) will want to be around them for any other reason than sheer necessity. The reason I know all these things is because I have struggled and continue to struggle with these negative emotions (from both winning and losing). Nevertheless, I can attest that Level 3 (the contributive/love) and Level 4 (the transcendent/spiritual life) help immeasurably to diminish the pain, emptiness, and obsession of a dominant Level 2 identity. Indeed, as will be seen, the spiritual life can break the grip of a dominant Level 2 identity and usher in a life of sublimity in God.

In Christian religious faith, "living on Level 4" means desiring the unconditionally loving, good, truth-filled, and salvific will of the unconditionally loving God. The proof and explanation of this unconditionally loving, good, truth-filled, and salvific will occurs through the revelation of Jesus Christ and the inspiration of the Holy Spirit.

An *intellectual* choice of Level 4 as one's fulfillment, purification, and joy does not necessarily translate into an *affective* (emotional) choice of Level 4. Thus, we might say that Level 4 is the identity to which we want to move, but find ourselves unable to give up attachments to Levels 1 and 2 (which interfere with the move to Level 4). We can therefore find ourselves in conflicts of desire, failures of resolve, and feelings of inadequacy and guilt. You should not find this daunting because it is part of *everyone's* journey toward Level 4. I am not aware of a single person (or a single saint) who found detachment from Levels 1 and 2 easy. However, patience, positive reinforcement, negative reinforcement, and, above all, prayer pave the way for progress. Slowly but surely Levels 3 and 4 begin to replace the deep attachment to Levels 1 and 2, bringing with them a decrease in jealousy, fear, anger, egocentricity, self-pity, contempt, inferiority, superiority, ego-sensitivity, and so many other debilitating emotive states. In their place, Level 4 (arising out of a deep relationship with the unconditionally loving God) brings peace, inspiration, zeal, hope, a remarkable efficacy in life, and above all, love (even progress toward unconditional Love). In short, the long journey of detachment from Levels 1 and 2 toward attachment to Levels 3 and 4 brings sanity, peace, and eternal Love.

As will by now be clear, the most effective way of moving from Levels 1 and 2 to Levels 3 and 4 is through God's grace, and the most effective way of allowing God's grace to affect us is through prayer and the contemplative life.

A Checklist for Growth in the Spiritual Life

The following five steps will lead to the purification of Level 4 desire, the presence of the Holy Spirit in our actions, a deepening of the Beatitudes in our hearts, the presence of God's grace leading to salvation, and the joy of life in Christ.

✓ Increase participation in the Holy Eucharist (perhaps attending Mass on Fridays during Lent, or even daily during Lent, Fridays throughout the year, or even daily throughout the year).

✓ Develop a list of spontaneous prayers—and use them.

✓ Make an Ignatian-style contemplative retreat. Set aside at least four days in the next year or two for this important step in building a contemplative base. Consider making another such retreat every year or every other year.

✓ Set aside fifteen minutes per day for daily prayer. Include time for:

- *Praise* (from the *Magnificat*, the *Word Among Us*, the breviary, and/or the Rosary), and

- *Gratitude* savored through the Examen prayer.

✓ Listen more attentively to the consolations and desolations
   of the loving God and the guidance of the Holy Spirit.

If the above steps are taken sincerely, your heart will be filled
with the heart of Jesus, which is the heart of the Beatitudes,
the heart of our destiny, and the heart of *Abba*, our Father.

References

Augustine, Saint. *Confessions.* Translated by Henry Chadwick. New York: Oxford University Press, 1991.

Bradley, Walter L. "Designed or Designoid?" In *Mere Creation: Science, Faith & Intelligent Design.* Edited by William A. Dembski. Downers Grove, Ill.: InterVarsity Press, 1998.

Brock, D. L. *Our Universe: Accident or Design?* Wits, South Africa: Star Watch Press, 1992.

Brown, Raymond. *An Introduction to New Testament Christology.* New York: Paulist Press, 1994.

Dunn, James D. G. *Jesus and the Spirit: A Study of the Religious and Charismatic Experience of Jesus and the First Christians as Reflected in the New Testament.* Philadelphia: The Westminster Press, 1975.

Frankl, Viktor. *Man's Search for Meaning: An Introduction to Logotherapy.* Translated by Ilse Lasch. Boston: Beacon Press, 1992.

———. *Man's Search for Ultimate Meaning.* Cambridge, Mass.: Perseus Publishing, 2000.

Gödel, Kurt. "Über formal unentscheidbare Sätze der Principia Mathematica und verwandter Systeme I." *Monatshefte für Mathematik und Physik* 38 (1931): 173–98.

Hoyle, Fred. *Engineering and Science.* Pasadena, Calif.: California Institute of Technology, 1981, pp. 8–12.

Ignatius of Loyola, Saint. *The Spiritual Exercises of St. Ignatius.* Translated by Louis J. Puhl. Chicago: Loyola University Press, 1951.

Jastrow, Robert. *God and the Astronomers.* New York: Warner Books, 1978.

John of the Cross, Saint. "The Living Flame of Love." *In The Collected Works of St. John of the Cross.* Translated by Kieran Kavanaugh and Otilio Rodriguez. Washington, D.C.: ICS Publications, 1979, pp. 569–649.

Lewis, C. S. *Surprised by Joy: The Shape of My Early Life.* New York: Harcourt, Brace and World, 1955.

Nouwen, Henri. *The Return of the Prodigal Son: A Story of Homecoming.* New York: Continuum, 1995.

Penrose, Roger. *The Emperor's New Mind.* Oxford: Oxford University Press, 1989.

Spitzer, Robert J. *The Spirit of Leadership: Optimizing Creativity and Change in Organizations.* Seattle, Wash.: Pacific Institute Publishing, 2000.

———. *Healing the Culture: A Commonsense Philosophy of Happiness, Freedom, and the Life Issues.* San Francisco: Ignatius Press, 2000.

———. "Proofs for the Existence of God, Part I: A Metaphysical Argument." *International Philosophical Quarterly* 41, no. 2, (June, 2001): 161–81.

———. "Proofs for the Existence of God, Part II." *International Philosophical Quarterly* 41, no. 3, (September, 2001): 305–31.

———. "Indications of Creation in Contemporary Big Bang Cosmology." *Philosophy in Science* 10 (2003): 35–106.

———. "Indications of Supernatural Design in Contemporary Big Bang Cosmology." *Ultimate Reality and Meaning* 27, no. 4 (2004): 265–87.

———. *New Proofs for the Existence of God: Contributions of Contemporary Physics and Philosophy.* A completed manuscript submitted for publication.

———. *Emmanuel: Evidence of the Unconditional Love of God and the Divinity of Jesus.* A completed manuscript.

Teresa of Avila, Saint. "The Book of Her Life." In *The Collected Works of St. Teresa of Avila.* Vol. 1. Translated by Kieran Kavanaugh and Otilio Rodriguez. Washington, D.C.: ICS Publications, 1976, pp. 31–308.

Underhill, Evelyn. *Mysticism: A Study in the Nature and Development of Man's Spiritual Consciousness.* London: Methuen, 1930.